THE ESSENTIAL GUIDE TO MOOTING

The Essential Guide to Mooting

A HANDBOOK FOR LAW STUDENTS

Emir Aly Crowne-Mohammed

Assistant Professor, University of Windsor, Faculty of Law,
Founder and Co-Chair of the Harold G. Fox Intellectual Property Moot

Mohamed R. Hashim

Articling Student (2009–2010), Heenan Blaikie LLP,
Law Clerk (2010–2011), Mr. Justice Hughes, Federal Court (Canada),
Co-founder of the Harold G. Fox Intellectual Property Moot

WITH AN APPENDIX ON DRAFTING MOTIONS BY
Shelley Kierstead

Assistant Professor, and Director of the Legal Research and Writing Program,
Osgoode Hall Law School

The Essential Guide to Mooting: A Handbook for Law Students
© Irwin Law Inc., 2010

Published in 2010 by

Irwin Law Inc.
14 Duncan Street
Suite 206
Toronto, ON
M5H 3G8

www.irwinlaw.com

ISBN: 978-1-55221-182-3

Cataloguing in Publication available from Library and Archives Canada

The publisher acknowledges the financial support of the Government of Canada through the Book Publishing Industry Development Program (BPIDP) for its publishing activities.

We acknowledge the assistance of the OMDC Book Fund, an initiative of Ontario Media Development Corporation.

Printed and bound in Canada.

1 2 3 4 5   14 13 12 11 10

Mixed Sources
Product group from well-managed forests, controlled sources and recycled wood or fiber
www.fsc.org Cert no. SW-COC-000952
© 1996 Forest Stewardship Council
FSC

Contents

Foreword

Professor Emir Aly Crowne-Mohammed and Mohamed R. Hashim are to be congratulated for their excellent book on mooting. As Canadian law schools continue to expand their mooting programs and increase the emphasis on moot participation, *The Essential Guide to Mooting: A Handbook for Law Students* will undoubtedly be of great value to their students.

For many law students, mooting is a new phenomenon and learning experience—the benefit of which will extend far beyond the courtroom. Mooting is an important step in the development of one's advocacy and communication skills. A "how-to" guide as thorough as this book provides students with a roadmap to crafting a successful career as a mooter, and future advocate in many different fora.

The authors have taken the time to analyse each aspect of mooting, from crafting to delivering arguments. It is their detailed consideration of the many facets of mooting that makes this a unique and worthwhile tool for mooters. Each area of the moot has been broken down into its own chapter, allowing the readers to distinguish it from the next. The moot is considered in its various phases: the preparatory stage; delivering opening and reply submissions; and questions from the bench. There are also other insightful chapters focusing on etiquette and presentation style.

After reading this book and using it as a guide, students will be better prepared to step into their "courtrooms" and present credible and persuasive arguments in a manner corresponding to the finest of advocacy skills. The result, I believe, will be that the calibre of mooting will only improve and continue to reflect the high quality of those behind the arguments: Canada's law students.

The Honourable Allan Lutfy,
Chief Justice of the Federal Court (Canada)

Why a Book on Mooting?

The immediate question that comes to mind for any reader is, why a book on **mooting**? There are dozens of quality writings on advocacy,[1] so what makes law school mooting special enough to deserve its own text?

Ask any law students preparing for their first year moot or a competitive moot competition — easily recognizable by their strained facial grimaces — and the need for a book such as this one is apparent: anyone who believes that advocacy tips for members of the bar can simply be transposed to student mooters without further qualification or refinement is naïve about the mooting process. Mooting is not "true" appellate advocacy, and law students are not practising members of the bar. While lawyers seek the best outcome for the clients (in the guise of the pursuit of justice), law students are seeking the best grades (or best outcome for their law school); thus, there are different considerations, duties, and obligations at stake.

This book seeks to provide those nuances that are unique to law school mooting. For this edition, we confine our tips and best practices to arguing motions and/or domestic, appellate level moots.[2]

Indeed, the moot advocacy tips and strategies set out in this book reflect the best practices gleaned from participating, coaching, organizing, and judging hundreds of appellate level moots. We can never remove the anxiety of mooting, but

---

1 See the Additional Readings set out in Appendix E.
2 Future editions will address some of the nuances of international moot competitions (like the Philip C Jessup International Law Moot Court Competition) or trial level moots (like the Arnup Cup).

we hope to increase the confidence of prospective mooters and provide a consistent baseline for mooters, coaches and judges to evaluate their performance.

Our focus will be on the art—and science—of mooting.[3]

---

3   There are many excellent works on factum preparation (and legal writing in general) already aimed at law students (for instance, Ted Tjaden's work, *Legal Research and Writing*, 2d ed. (Toronto: Irwin Law, 2004)). These are set out (with an asterisk) in the Additional Readings in Appendix E. Professor Shelley Kierstead has also set out some tips in Appendix D on drafting persuasive Motions.

Acknowledgments

The authors would like to thank their families—Liana Dass, Sonja Moham-med, Sara Mohammed, Mohamed Hashim (Sr.), Bibi Hashim, and Shaun Hashim—for their loving support and encouragement.

We would also like to thank the members of the Harold G. Fox Intellectual Property Moot Committee for making the inaugural (2009) Moot a success—Chief Justice Allan Lutfy, Justice Edgar Sexton, Justice Eleanore Cronk, Ron Dimock, Bruce Stratton, Angela Furlanetto, and Cristina Mihalceanu.

A special acknowledgement also goes out to the Federal Court (Canada) and the Ontario Court of Appeal for the many moots they host and support each year.

CHAPTER 1

Setting the Scene: Modern Mooting

In its earliest form, mooting can be traced as far back as 1485 CE when it was organized by centres of legal education — the Inns of Court.[1] As is the case now, moots were used to teach law students the details of oral advocacy and to provide a forum to refine their skills through situational practice.[2]

Mooting is usually a mandatory requirement for first-year law students. Moots have regained their significance in the "black letter" world of legal academia, as a means of exposing students to the clinical and experiential aspects of the legal profession. In Canada alone there are forty-two competitive moots ranging from in-house events to national and international contests.[3]

First-year moots are structured either as a motion[4] or as an appeal to a "supreme" moot court.[5] Likewise, most competitive moots are structured as appeals of either a trial level decision or appeals before an otherwise "supreme" moot court.[6] This is done for organizational simplicity, and explains the focus of

---

1 Tim Kaye & Lynne Townley, *Blackstone's Book of Moots* (Glasgow: Bell & Bain Limited, 1996) 3.
2 Of course, the doctrinal and academic function of the Inns has largely been replaced by law schools.
3 Julius Melnitzer, "Law School Mooting" *Lexpert Magazine* (25 April 2009) online: Lexpert www.lexpert.ca/Magazine/GlobeAndMail.aspx.
4 Professor Shelley Kierstead has provided some guidance on drafting persuasive motions (for first-year moots). These are set out in Appendix D.
5 These are usually graded on a pass/fail basis. Some first-year moots also provide the opportunity for the mooter to pass with distinction or pass with honours.
6 Students usually receive academic credit for participation in competitive moots. Credit is usually assessed through a combination of factors (some more subjective than others). For instance, grades can be assigned solely on the student's oral performance on the day(s) of the moot. It can also be a mixture of the student's oral performance, factum quality, teamwork,

this book. It is simpler to argue an appeal on a point of law than it is in a mock trial with the requisite cross-examination of witnesses and other procedural requirements. While mock trials are more common among US law schools, some full-scale mock trials at the competitive level do exist.[7] A sample **moot problem** from the inaugural 2009–2010 Harold G. Fox Intellectual Property Moot is set out in Appendix A.

As an exercise in appellate advocacy, most moots feature a pair of students representing the **Appellant** and a pair representing the **Respondent**. Some moots also include a fifth student who may act as an alternate mooter or otherwise assist the moot team(s) with research, preparation, and other remedial tasks. Most moot competitions forbid any involvement of professors, practitioners, or other experts in the preparation of each pair's factum.[8] Aside from the general assistance of librarians and similar professionals, law students must become subject matter experts and direct their own research, writing, and learning. In terms of oral argumentation, the appellant pair makes their **submissions** first, followed by the respondent pair. Each individual mooter is permitted between ten to thirty minutes of time for argumentation, depending on the competition's rules. The appellant pair is usually offered a **right of reply**, with a time limit of two to five minutes, depending on the competition's rules.

It is also true that law students are often coached by their student peers — either from within the **moot team** itself, or other law students. Law professors and practitioners are simply unavailable to coach and mentor students with any regularity. Indeed, as a courtesy (and as a matter of pride), student mooters often do not seek the mentorship and coaching of their professors or external practitioners until they have "graduated" past their peers.

Moot coaches are the formal coaches of the moot team. They can generally be characterized by three distinct personality types or models — the expert, the mentor, and the administrator.

The expert is usually a professor with in-depth subject matter expertise. The expert will provide guidance on oral advocacy and factum writing (although, mooters should be aware that some competitions forbid this type of direct involvement). The expert will pigeonhole the moot problem to match her particular subject matter niche. Student mooters will often be pressed with multiple rounds of intense, micromanaged coaching. The expert will expect (and directly supervise) more than ten rounds of practice.

The mentor is also a subject matter expert, but he views his role to be that of a "sounding board" or facilitator. He provides the subject matter expertise for

---

and preparation. Most competitive moots release the mooters' oral scores and factum scores to aid in this grading.

7   Like the Ontario Trial Lawyers Association Cup and Arnup Cup.

8   The rules from the 2009–2010 Harold G. Fox Intellectual Property Moot are set out in Appendix C for reference.

the mooters to launch their own research. The mentor will occasionally assist in judging practice rounds, but prefers to see the students take charge and arrange these matters. The mentor will expect (but not necessarily supervise) up to ten rounds of practice.

The administrator is merely a coach "on paper." She provides little assistance or guidance to mooters. Sometimes this is due to lack of subject matter expertise or a lack of interest.[9] The administrator has no expectations as to the number of rounds of practice.

Experience has shown that the mentor model is the most effective in moot preparation. A balance must be struck between formal and peer coaches. **Peer coaching** and peer feedback are essential aspects of moot preparation. It should not be discouraged. Nor should "peer coaching" be artificially created through micromanagement by the formal coach. Mooters have egos. They have a sense of pride. All moot teams—even ones led by an administrator—instinctively arrange their affairs based on the peer coaching model. Intrinsic to this model is the emergence of a "**leader**" from within the moot team itself. Sometimes this can be difficult for the other team members (or the formal coach) to accept, but it must happen. In the most successful teams, there is a strong bond between this leader and the formal coach, built on a mutual level of respect and desire to reach common goals. Without this, the relationship devolves into the expert or administrator model.

Peer coaching is also intrinsically useful in learning to withstand criticism from one's peers. Student mooters who can respond intelligently and with dignity to a panel of their fellow teammates (or other law students) will be well-equipped for dealing with a panel of practitioners or members of the judiciary on the day of the moot itself.

Peer coaching—or more specifically, peer judging—also allows mooters to gain valuable insight into the mind of a moot judge. Indeed, every once in a while an article or speech is given by a judge on the topic of "what I would have done differently if I knew then what I know now."[10] When student mooters act as judges during practice rounds, there is a new-found appreciation for the bench. Student mooters who act as moot judges soon develop a keen sense of what "works" and what does not when it comes to advocacy. Keeping a bench "interested" is, after all, the reason why we still rely on oral argumentation (as

---

9 The harsh reality is that many professors are mandated to coach moot teams as part of their administrative service to their law schools. There is often no direction (or choice) given to moot coaches as to the proper management and training of moot teams. Additionally, practitioner coaches—perhaps understandably—often sacrifice diligent supervision of their moot team in favour of billable work.

10 See, for example, The Honourable Justice John I. Laskin, "The View from the Other Side: What I Would Have Done Differently if I Knew Then What I Know Now" (Spring 1998) 17:2 Advocates' Soc. J. 16.

opposed to relying only on written submissions). Moot judging is an absolute "must" in order to develop a taste for the "other side."

Early in the practice rounds — usually around the third practice (when the moot team has ironed out its submissions and is beginning to get comfortable with them) — the formal coach should arrange a **Hard Panel**. The Hard Panel's job is to test the mettle of the team's submissions by actively questioning each mooter's submissions with daunting scepticism. The Hard Panel is the "wake-up call." It eliminates the false sense of security and preparedness that many mooters develop. The Hard Panel should consist of the formal coach and two to four professors, practitioners, or members of the judiciary. Mooters should be told that the panel will indeed go "hard," and they should be reminded that they should not take this part of the learning curve personally. The Hard Panel, in turn, should also be informed that they should be constructive, not destructive, in their criticism. All too often we have seen Hard Panels that expect mooters to explain why the moot problem's factual record is incomplete, or otherwise become overly concerned with purely doctrinal aspects of the moot problem. This is irrelevant and unhelpful. Instead, the Hard Panel should be painfully fastidious about the points of law.

At the conclusion of the Hard Panel, mooters should again be reminded by the panellists that none of the panel's attacks are personal, nor are they intended to demean. The Hard Panel's job is to completely shake the foundation of a team's submissions. Mooters should use the session as an opportunity to rebuild their submissions and make them stronger. Future practice rounds should feature moderately active panellists in order to test the efficacy and value of the Hard Panel.[11]

These are the basics of the "organizational management" of the moot team. In the following chapters we look at the different types of argumentation available to a mooter, the basics of structuring one's submissions, and dealing with questions from the bench.

---

11 The Hard Panel is, after all, intended to represent the "worst case scenario" for the team, and moderately active panels will likely be closer to the norm on the actual day(s) of the moot competition.

The Essential Guide to Mooting

CHAPTER 2

Preparation

As an academic exercise, moots are intended to give the "feel" of a live legal case. Moots, for better or worse, reflect the *Law and Order* vision that most students have of law school. And, just like Jack McCoy on the fictional television series (now replaced by the natty Mike Cutter), the key to success in a competitive moot is preparation.[1] Strategic preparation is a constant theme for students throughout law school—from course selection to on-campus interviews—and mooting is no different. A student must approach this task with focus and dedication. All mooters experience some anxiety (especially those who claim they do not). In fact, a mooter without anxiety is no longer an *advocate*, she is merely a student. Anxiety connotes a sense of passion and conviction.

While there are many individual styles or methods to moot preparation, a number of traits and principles appear consistent among top mooters. Top mooters *believe* they are appellate lawyers. They understand the theatrics involved. They are playing a role. Justice Pomerance, of the Ontario Court of Justice, aptly distils appellate preparation into three broad categories: (1) developing a mastery of the facts; (2) forming a clear structure/outline of argument; and (3)

---

1   David Stockwood, "Remembering John Robinette" (2003) 22:2 Advocates' Soc. J. 1 (citing John J. Robinette Q.C. who was quoted as saying: "You win by preparation and drudgery. You do research and you read. The actual appearance in court is often like the tip of an iceberg. [You] try to be succinct. [You] formulate your argument as concisely yet as effectively as possible, getting down to the point of the case, avoiding red herrings. Sometimes it means weeks of preparation." (*The Globe and Mail* (26 November 1979)).

crafting an effective opening remark.[2] It is important to explore each of these elements at length.

Mastering the facts of a particular moot problem is vital to success. Appellate moot problems are drafted to provide fodder for both appellant and respondent. In well-drafted moot problems, there is rarely an irrelevant fact nor are the issues overwhelmingly one-sided. The facts for a moot problem are located in the trial decision. Judgements often contain sections where the trial judge will make "findings of fact." These findings of fact are central to the legal arguments that a mooter will make, and students must know these facts inside and out.

During moots, it is essential that student mooters respect these findings of "fact." These facts are not to be disturbed. Even in practice, these facts are rarely disturbed by higher Courts.[3] The Supreme Court of Canada itself has emphasized the deference owed to a trial judge's findings of fact:

> [A]ppellate courts are not in a favourable position to assess and determine factual matters. Appellate court judges are restricted to reviewing written transcripts of testimony. As well, appeals are unsuited to reviewing voluminous amounts of evidence. Finally, appeals are telescopic in nature, focussing narrowly on particular issues as opposed to viewing the case as a whole.[4]

Remember, moot competitions are academic exercises that are intended to expose students to the practical application of the law. Appellate moot competitions are tests of a student's ability to blend doctrine, oration, style, and gumption. In oral submissions, a student must never attempt to retry the facts of the moot problem because it aggravates the bench. An aggravated bench will either launch into irrelevant (and distracting) questions, or otherwise be too sidetracked to absorb the mooter's core submissions.

A student must digest the facts as they are, and accept them as absolute. Again, even in practice, a trial judge's findings of fact will never be disrupted except in instances of a "palpable and overriding error."[5] Therefore, in a moot competition, an argument seeking to retry the facts is useless and should be avoided. Preparation should be focused on crafting and manipulating those

---

2   The Honourable Justice Renee M. Pomerance, "Appellate Advocacy: Presenting the Oral Argument" (May 2002) online: The Supreme Court Advocacy Institute www.scai-ipcs.ca/pdf/Pomerance-PreentingtheOralArgument.pdf.

3   "The appellate court must not re-try a case and must not substitute its views for the views of the trial judge according to what the appellate court thinks the evidence establishes on its view of the balance of probabilities." (*Underwood v. Ocean City Realty Ltd.* (1987), 12 B.C.L.R. (2d) 199 at 204 (C.A.)).

4   *Housen v. Nikolaisen*, 2002 SCC 33 at para. 14.

5   *Ibid.* at para. 120. See also *Stein v. The Ship "Kathy K"*, [1976] 2 S.C.R. 802 at 808; *Ingles v. Tutkaluk Construction Ltd.*, [2000] 1 S.C.R. 298 at para. 42; *Ryan v. Victoria (City)*, [1999] 1 S.C.R. 201 at para. 57; and *Resurfice Corp. v. Hanke*, 2007 SCC 7 at para. 10.

facts in one's favour; remember, a strong mooter can manipulate facts without seeming manipulative. The Supreme Court of Canada has even acknowledged this skill in appellate advocacy:

> While few counsel would claim Shakespearean powers of persuasion, the fact remains that in an age burdened with "spin doctors" it should be unnecessary to belabour the point that the same underlying facts can be used to create very different impressions depending on the advocacy skills of counsel.[6]

The facts are only as strong as the intensity of the light a mooter shines on them. For instance, a moot problem may indicate that 500,000 people did not receive medical care based on income, gender, disability, and age. A mooter who represented the class of individuals denied medical care might emphasize that "half a million" Canadians are without medical care; "half a million poor, disabled, and elderly Canadians." Alternatively, if the mooter represented the governmental authority responsible for administering (or denying) the medical care, the student might state that "*about* one percent" of Canadians are denied medical care; "this is no more than a *de minimis* amount." "Facts" are rarely factual.

Stemming from this is Justice Pomerance's second guideline to appellate preparation — the legal argument. When structuring her argument, the student should approach this task methodically to create full and sound oral submissions. A student in a moot court, just like a practising lawyer, must have a sound understanding of the minutia of a case since a panel of judges will demand "a keen appreciation of *both* the forest *and* the trees."[7] To gain this understanding, we must examine the various avenues of argumentation available. Generally, there are three. Mooters can structure their arguments based on the law, equity, or policy. Usually, it is a skilful blend of the first two that tends to win the day.

Arguments grounded in law are based on a strict or contextual interpretation of the applicable jurisprudence. Traditional examples can be broken down into simple "if/then" situations. For instance, if an individual drives in excess of the designated speed limit in a community safety zone, the fine levied will be double the standard prescribed fee, in accordance with subsection 214.1(6) of Ontario's *Highway Traffic Act*.[8] A legal argument would apply the usual canons of statutory interpretation (is Ontario's *Highway Traffic Act* to be interpreted strictly? Purposively? What is the mischief that it seeks to remedy?) to the fact that the individual drove above the speed limit in a community safety zone.

Equitable arguments, by their very nature, provide more flexibility than merely picking between canons of statutory interpretation. If equity ameliorates

---

6   *R. v. Rose*, [1998] 3 S.C.R. 262 at para. 19.

7   Pomerance, above note 2.

8   R.S.O. 1990, c. H.8.

the common law's harshness, then depending on one's position as either an appellant or respondent, there is always scope for at least one party to seek relief from the law's austerity. Ever since the ancient *Judicature Acts* fused the common law courts with courts of equity, there has been no doubt that first instance courts (let alone appellate courts) can entertain arguments grounded in equity. For instance, Section 96 of the Ontario *Courts of Justice Act*[9] explicitly provides that equitable arguments can be heard in Ontario's courts. Indeed, subsection 96(2) of the Ontario *Courts of Justice Act* has codified the long-standing rule that "[w]here a rule of equity conflicts with a rule of the common law, the rule of equity prevails."[10] An effective and prepared mooter must therefore identify the conflict in the law—where a strict (or even purposive) application would cause an unjust result—and urge the Court to adopt an equitable solution.[11]

The last avenue of argumentation is the most delicate (and perhaps the most fanciful). Policy arguments are not based on law or equity. Policy arguments have their roots in a subjective understanding of how the law "ought" to function. For instance, although the *Youth Criminal Justice Act*[12] contains provisions that are designed to protect youth between the ages of twelve and eighteen from being tried in an adult court, a policy argument may be made that deterring violent, young, repeat offenders is adequate justification for an adult trial.

However, there is a real danger in using policy arguments, especially if policy arguments are arguments about how the law "ought" to operate. Naturally, the law "ought" to operate in favour of the mooter's position. Therefore, for every policy argument that can be made, there is always a corresponding counter argument of equal merit. In the above example, to rebut the policy argument

---

9 R.S.O. 1990, c. C.43.
10 *Ibid.*
11 The equitable maxims that might be of most assistance to mooters are as follows:
   1. Equity regards as done that which ought to be done.
   2. Equity will not suffer a wrong to be without a remedy.
   3. Equity delights in equality.
   4. One who seeks equity must do equity.
   5. Equity aids the vigilant, not those who slumber on their rights.
   6. Equity imputes an intent to fulfill an obligation.
   7. Equity acts *in personam*.
   8. Equity does not require an idle gesture.
   9. One who comes into equity must come with clean hands.
   10. Equity delights to do justice and not by halves.
   11. Equity follows the law.
   12. Between equal equities the law will prevail.
   13. Between equal equities the first in order of time shall prevail.
   14. Equity will not complete an imperfect gift.
   15. Equity will not allow a statute to be used as a cloak for fraud.
12 S.C. 2002, c. 1.

on deterrence, a counter argument would assert that kids[13] carry a diminished moral blameworthiness on account of their age.[14]

In a moot, policy arguments should never be the main thrust of one's submissions. Moots are won on a mastery of the facts and the application of the law or equity to those facts. When crafting one's oral submissions, a student should only invoke policy concerns to supplement their primary legal or equitable arguments. Indeed, policy arguments may be viewed by some panellists on a moot bench as a red herring (and by "red herring" we mean a sign that the student has neither researched nor thought about the law carefully enough). The late Justice Catzman, formerly of the Ontario Court of Appeal, wrote a classic article on "How to Lose Appeals in the Court of Appeal."[15] The article is as humorous as it is insightful and honest. Policy arguments were framed as follows:

> Judges love policy, because it makes them feel important. They can talk policy forever. Keep their minds away from the crucial words on which your appeal turns by talking instead about the need to adopt "a purposive approach" to whatever area of law you are discussing. That will effectively focus their attention where it belongs, and will almost certainly ensure defeat.[16]

This is where career academics might diverge from the advice of judges and practitioners. Law professors love policy. It is, after all, what most of them write about during their summer months. But Justice Catzman's admonition about policy arguments is undoubtedly correct. In a moot, a policy argument should only be used (if at all) to bolster an already sound set of oral submissions grounded in fact, law, and perhaps equity.

A few tips on general strategy. When structuring legal arguments, a student should carefully examine the trial decision in a moot problem. In ruling one way or another, a fictional judgement, like a real judgement, will inevitably shed light on the strengths and weaknesses of one side or another.

---

13   Notice we have intentionally used the word "kids" here instead of "youth." The notion of a "kid" being tried as an adult carries more emotive baggage than a "youth" on trial. The subtle and emotive use of language is a talent that is quite useful in some moots, especially moots which involve human rights or *Charter* issues. By the same token, moots that involve sterile corporate, commercial, or intellectual property disputes are often not the best avenues to advance emotive sentiment. The "pain and oppression" of a minority shareholder in an oppression remedy case is less stirring than the "pain and oppression" of a marginalized or minority group in a section 15 analysis under the *Charter of Rights and Freedoms*.

14   The policy debate on the blameworthiness of a young offender was a critical issue—one of a few that divided the Supreme Court of Canada—in the 5:4 decision of *R. v. D.B.*, 2008 SCC 25.

15   Marvin Catzman, "The Wrong Stuff: How to Lose Appeals in the Court of Appeal" (2000) 18:1 Advocates' Soc. J. 1.

16   *Ibid.* at 3–5.

The importance of the "facts" found by the trial judge is amplified on appeal, since these facts are not to be contested.[17] This may indirectly work to the advantage of the winner at trial. It is here that a student's work begins. If the mooter represents the party successful at trial, then she will often frame the facts as closely as possible to that of the trial judge. If the mooter represents the unsuccessful party at trial, she will either emphasize how the appeal judgment (if any) framed the facts, or manipulate the facts so that they are "read down" or narrowly considered.

Moot problems—that is, the trial judgments or appeal judgments (if available)—will inevitably cite case law, statute, or international instruments (if applicable). These primary sources represent the springboard for the student's legal research. The cases should be noted up to determine their treatment by subsequent courts. Students should know these cases inside and out. They are the baseline for the student's submissions. They will either need to be emphasized, distinguished, or memorized for one's oral submissions—especially since most moots deal with the (mis)application or (mis)interpretation of primary legal sources. A firm grasp of their applicability will often signal a mastery of the subject area to the judging panel.

With these preliminary points in mind—a mastery of both the facts and the law by the student—a strong foundation has been set for successful advocacy. From this point onward, the task is to deliver this blend of fact and law in a seamless, persuasive, and respectful manner.

---

17 On earlier pages, we have made it painfully clear that mooters should never contest or retry facts.

CHAPTER 3

Opening Remarks

The Court: "How are you going to divide the argument, Mr. Genest?"

Mr. Genest: "My Lords, unless I drop dead, I'm going to do it all."

Mr. Justice Beetz: "What did he say?"

Mr. Justice Estey: "He has reserved the right to die."[1]

When crafting an opening remark, students must be keenly aware of the importance placed on an effective introduction. In advocacy, an opening remark is a harbinger of the overall submissions. It must be simple (but not trite), informative (but not protracted), and compelling (but not melodramatic). This is no easy task. It requires deliberation, planning, and practice.

In effect, a student mooter must demonstrate command over her legal argument by introducing it to the panel of judges in an efficient manner. Reduced to two simple propositions an advocate must "[m]ake the court want to decide in [her] favour"; and then, "[s]how it how to do so."[2]

As Justice John I. Laskin notes:

Judges do not listen passively; they are always looking to make sense of what they are hearing. As advocates, you have to give them the context. So before you throw

---

1   The Honourable Justice Sopinka, "Appellate Advocacy" (March 1992) 11:1 Advocates' Soc. J. 16 at 18.

2   John W. Morden, "The Partnership of Bench and Bar" (David B. Goodman Memorial Lecture) (1982) 16 L. Soc'y Gaz. 46 at 72.

a lot of information and a lot of detail at a judge, begin with the point of the detail, the context for it, even your conclusion, not the other way around.[3]

An effective opening remark should typically be delivered within one to three minutes. It must relay the basic premise of what the student will be speaking about for the next ten to thirty minutes[4]. The opening remarks must be organized and clear, as "[g]ood advocates do not leave the judge in a state of confuzzlement."[5]

Effective opening remarks consist of a series of short, crisp statements. A strong introduction will serve a mooter extremely well for the remainder of their submissions. Justice Sopinka has characterized it well:

> The most telling characteristic of a bad counsel is the failure to begin with a prepared opening statement. A short and crisp opening statement lifts counsel from mediocrity to a higher level . . . . Its purpose is to draw a road map for the trier of fact. The main pitfall to avoid is overstating your case or giving too much detail. This leads to invidious comparisons with the case that is presented.[6]

A court is looking for a clear characterization of what is before them. A mooter must not pretend his case is larger or more significant than it truly is. A (moot) court may be a place of theatrics, but not melodramatics.

In the case of *Nelles v. Ontario*,[7] Justice Sopinka (in his days before he was a judge) went before the Supreme Court of Canada and delivered the following opening statement:

> My Lords and My Ladies,
>
> In this case the Court of Appeal has decided that crown attorneys enjoy immunity from civil suits. That makes them unique among public servants. The common law has uniformly refused to recognize any protection from civil liability for a public servant who has acted maliciously, but the Court of Appeal says it made one exception.[8]

---

3   The Honourable Justice John I. Laskin, "What Persuades (or, What's Going on Inside the Judge's Mind)" (Summer 2004) 23:1 Advocates' Soc. J. 4 at para. 19.

4   Depending on the time allotted to each student, or each team, as per the moot competition's rules.

5   See the remarks of the Honourable Justice Blair, "Oral Advocacy in Matters Argued Before Superior Court Judges" (1999) 18:2 Advocates' Soc. J. 26 at 26, where he whimsically adopts the term "confuzzlement" from the storybook character Winnie the Pooh. Pooh states that he is confuzzled, which Christopher Robin explains as being "sort of mixed up and baffled."

6   The Honourable Justice John Sopinka, "The Many Faces of Advocacy" (1990) 9:1 Advocates' Soc. J. 3 at 16.

7   [1989] 2 S.C.R. 170.

8   Sopinka, "Appellate Advocacy," above note 1 at 18.

Aside from the understandably dated salutation,[9] this statement has all of the hallmarks of a clean, crisp opening. There are four critical elements—a salutation, an introductory statement, a road map, and an order sought. As a template, consider the following example:

The Salutation:	Good afternoon Justices, my name is [first and last name] and I appear on behalf of the Respondent, [Respondent name].
The Introduction:	The thrust of my submissions today focuses on [the statutory provision impugned, or triggered, in the case at bar].
A Road Map:	I would like to take a brief moment and outline for you the structure of my submissions today [insert the basic premise of the one to three[10] submissions prepared].
Order Sought:	Now it is the Respondent's position that when these points are assessed and the facts of this case are taken into consideration there is [the conclusion being sought or asserted]. As a result, it is submitted that this appeal must be dismissed and the decision of the Court of Appeal upheld.

The first two elements are self-explanatory; however, the **road map** and order sought have strategic importance and require further elaboration.

A road map is the most basic—yet most effective—tool for an advocate. A road map sets out the chronological order of a mooter's submissions. It helps the panel to organize the multiple issues that are often interwoven into most moot problems. As Wendy Matheson states, "defining the issues can influence the outcome of the case. It is an opportunity, not a burden. Through the selection and articulation of the issues, you set out a road map that compels the court to follow your theory of the case, to your desired outcome."[11]

The "order sought" is also useful in a moot setting. Nearly all moot competitions focus on substantive legal issues; there are few (if any) moots that require students to explain the costs sought or sentencing period(s). Many moot court judges make the mistake of asking (or expecting) that students will indeed ad-

---

9 Terminology and phrases will be discussed later.

10 The ideal number of submissions will be discussed later in the paper, but experience shows that any itemization beyond three submissions tends to be forgotten or blurred in the panel's memory.

11 Wendy Matheson, "Keys to Successful Oral Advocacy: One View from the Bar" (Autumn 2007) 26:2 Advocates' Soc. J. 9 at para. 12. Matheson also makes the insightful remark that "clear oral advocacy has many of the hallmarks of clear written advocacy:

- Begin by telling the court where you are going. (Create a road map.)
- Keep that map as simple as possible. (Show the easiest way to get to your destination.)
- Use overt structure as much as possible. (Describe your map.)
- Distil your argument into simple propositions that convey the theory of your case." (*Ibid.* at para. 14.)

dress these matters. The "order sought" statement in a moot, therefore, refocuses the court's attention to the true crux or merits of the problem. Accordingly, as a general rule, students should reduce their position to one broad threshold question. If a decision can be succinctly reduced to a specific cause or outcome, judges will be far more receptive to it. On some level, judges are minimalists. They cannot decide everything. Indeed, "[j]udges like to resolve the dispute in front of them, and they don't mind leaving many things undecided. They prefer to say as little as possible to justify the result."[12]

Fuelled by the notion that a judge will likely accept a threshold question as the only issue to be resolved, a mooter would do well to present the remainder of the case in an equally straightforward manner. Indeed, having formulated the submissions as well as the introduction, the pivotal task becomes the delivery. The aim is to be compelling and persuasive.

---

12   Laskin, "What Persuades," above note 3 at 7.

CHAPTER 4

Delivering Submissions

"Be brief, be clear, be gone!"[1] — The Honourable Justice Estey

Competitive moots are judged largely on the basis of one's oral advocacy. Since the competitors in a moot are all working from a common moot problem (accompanied by the limited evidentiary record provided by the trial judgment), the actual merits of the case are, or ought to be, of little relevance to the judges. And, rightly or not, the factum is also given less weight than the actual oral submissions since the emphasis in moot competitions is the actual moot performance itself.

When delivering submissions, it is important to develop a strategy prior to taking the podium. The delivery of submissions should demonstrate a quiet confidence to the judges. Be prepared. In this sense, oral advocacy is no different than written advocacy. An advocate would never submit the first draft of a factum, nor should a mooter present a rough and unrehearsed set of submissions.

The key to the successful delivery of oral submissions is the structure employed by the advocate. A student must prepare a script that allows for easy transitions between one's submissions and the questions from the bench. Unlike a theatre script, this script is not intended to be read verbatim — nor should it. Oral submissions are not a recital of the factum; judges can read.

---

1   The Honourable Justice Estey, as quoted by John J.L. Hunter, Q.C. in "Presenting a Civil Appeal" at 13.3.23–24. (Paper presented at C.L.E. Advocacy Symposium, Vancouver, British Columbia, November 2001) [unpublished].

Submissions should be viewed as a structured conversation with the bench. It is a conversation that is initiated by the mooter, but is directed by the bench. Justice Binnie has framed it well:

> [D]on't be too rigid in your conception of the argument. Unlike a normal, everyday jury, you didn't select the jurors; they selected you and your case because there are issues in it they want to address. If you're a good advocate, you won't necessarily talk about what you want to talk about; you'll talk about what they want to talk about. You may think they've misread the "real point." If so, that's their problem. Your problem is to win the case.[2]

One's script must therefore be organized in a manner that maximizes a mooter's ability to move in and out with fluidity. The overall structure should align with the factum but should never be a mirror image. Indeed, a typical mistake made by many mooters (and their coaches) is the zealous recitation of the facts. This not only wastes precious time, it also aggravates the panel of practitioners or judicial members who have volunteered their time to the moot competition. The bench is aware of the facts. Indeed, even a panellist who may have skimmed a mooter's factum has still read the moot problem (or has been provided with a bench brief[3] by the organizers of the moot competition).

Reciting a lengthy quotation[4] is another advocacy mistake, especially those passages that establish "what the law is" or "where the law originates." If the quotation is in the mooter's factum, then leave it there. It does not need to be reread. Just direct the Court's attention to that particular paragraph (or tab in the book of authorities, if there is one). If the quotation is extraneous, leave it there as well. Do not use lengthy quotations in your submissions. If submissions are to be viewed as a structured conversation, then quoting someone else is hardly an effective means of raising their own standing in the panel's mind. Indeed, the verbatim recitation of someone else's words places the mooter outside of this conversation. If a mooter insists on using a quotation, try to avoid "olde" English judgments. No one says "ye" anymore; everyone knows about the *Judicature Acts*; Latin impresses no one. Indeed, "[w]here a passage *is* to be read, it should be identified in advance, and kept as brief as possible."[5]

---

2   The Honourable Justice Ian Binnie, "A Survivor's Guide to Advocacy in the Supreme Court of Canada" (1999) 18:2 Advocates' Soc. J. 13 at 16.

3   A bench brief is a memo prepared by the organizers of a moot that distils the problem to the bare essentials. It will often include case law and potential arguments as well as sample questions for the jurists to ask.

4   For convenience sake, we consider anything longer than two sentences (or anything that takes more than 20 seconds to say) to be a "lengthy" quotation.

5   The Honourable Justice Renee M. Pomerance, "Appellate Advocacy: Presenting the Oral Argument" (May 2002) online: The Supreme Court Advocacy Institute www.scai-ipcs.ca/pdf/Pomerance-PresentingtheOralArgument.pdf at 10.

With an ever increasing list of "do nots" in delivering submissions, students should not lose sight of the ultimate objective of traditional oral advocacy — representing the client to the best of the mooter's abilities. In the traditional judicial setting, the merits of the case tend to win the day. However, for moot judges, the merits of the moot problem are not important. It may be true that the best mooters also happen to win their case, but this is not necessarily true. Moots are academic exercises, and moot judges are keen to see students demonstrate equal measures of creativity, poise, and preparation.

When preparing arguments for delivery, it is useful to adhere to the **Rule of Three.** In approaching a moot problem, the natural impulse is to devise as many arguments as possible in the hope that something "sticks." This impulse is misguided and counterproductive. It demonstrates a lack of discipline and a lack of prioritization. A mooter who announces to the panel that she will be making seven submissions (or even five submissions) will invariably lose the attention and patience of the bench. Indeed, the panel may absorb the first few submissions, but the later submissions would become lost amongst the panellist's other thoughts. Moreover, multiple submissions may cause a strong first submission to become diluted when accompanied by several other weaker (and perhaps distracting) submissions. The "magic" number of submissions appears to be three or less. Narrowing (or grouping) one's arguments into two or three solid points demonstrates a keen sense of prioritization and time management. Justice Finlayson even endorses the Rule of Three for "real" litigation:

> In any given case, the most significant issues cannot number more than three. As an aide memoire to be attached to every counsel's brief, permit me to state unequivocally that no judge in a single trial has made more than three reversible errors. Counsel may think the judge has made many more, and the panel members may have their own thoughts, but that is an impermissible thought process for the true advocate. Three is the outside number for judicial purposes. Look at it this way: the appellant needs to establish only one reversible error to succeed, and the "rule of three" gives counsel three chances to achieve that result. If counsel proceeds to argue that there are more errors than that, counsel is acknowledging failure with respect to the first three.[6]

The Rule of Three should not be used as a tactic to completely ignore a mooter's weaker arguments, especially if one of those arguments pertains directly to the issue(s) to be decided on appeal. Rather, a direct approach is most useful. Address weak points or contentious issues "head on" to prevent negative inferences from being drawn by the bench. As Justice Pomerance notes:

---

6   The Honourable Justice George Finlayson, "Appellate Advocacy in an Abbreviated Setting" (1999) 18:2 Advocates' Soc. J. 22 at 23.

Wilful blindness is no more helpful to the advocate than it is to the person charged with possession of stolen property. One can generally assume that hidden warts and imperfections will be happily exposed by one's opponent, or worse yet, the court. When this happens, the potential harm can extend beyond the case and injure the advocate's most precious commodity—his or her credibility.[7]

Mooters should sandwich their weaker issue(s) in the middle of their three submissions. Why? Because it leaves the opening argument, and the closing argument as the strongest (and most memorable) aspects of a mooter's performance.

As a general point of advocacy, students should not use all three of their submissions to rebut arguments raised against them, nor should a student spend all of her allotted time rebutting every argument she anticipates from the opponent. This is not an effective use of time. Rather than rebut, a student should use her three submissions to advance an argument. In doing so, judges are guided to focus on the positive elements of her position. A savvy tactician does not spend a significant amount of time anticipating and discussing an opponent's submissions. This smacks of desperation and uncertainty. It also highlights the strength of the opponent's arguments and encourages the panel to focus more on the points *against* rather than *for*.

Following the Rule of Three, the next skill is persuasive delivery. Of course, there is no magic formula that guarantees success at a moot. However, there are some best practices that mooters can employ to enhance the delivery of their submissions (and their overall performance).

First, be yourself. Every mooter has his own style. Pretending to be more formal or more aggressive usually results in an out-of-character performance which is easily discernible by the bench. If the advocate is insincere, so are his submissions. Even though students are playing a "role" when mooting, they are still themselves. They are actors in *their own* plays. Delivering submissions based on one's personal style will ensure a smooth and fluid performance. Sincerity breeds sincerity.

Second, consider the importance of **inflection**. Everyone can inject inflection into her voice. The value of inflection lies in the subtle—yet assertive—emphasis it places on key points. It serves as an unconscious cue for judges to focus on these points. By contrast, a monotone delivery—as most law students are aware during lectures—does not leave a positive or memorable impression. (Remember, a mooter is judged, *inter alia*, on how memorable her performance was relative to the other participants.) So, how does a mooter become memorable (in the right way)?

Third, develop a common theme or strand throughout one's submissions. Often referred to as a "narrative," or core theory, this is basically a catchphrase

---

7   Above note 5 at 10.

that sums up the essence of a mooter's position.[8] This is a mooter's "**Waldo.**"[9] The Waldo is a mooter's safety. It is the one phrase that summarizes the essence of a mooter's position. Waldos also serve as a neat and clean way of answering a question from the bench and tying it back to the mooter's submissions. For instance, in a moot problem dealing with the abuse of process at an extradition hearing, the Waldo for mooters representing the accused may be the lack of a "meaningful judicial process."[10] When questioned by the panel, a mooter must still respond intelligently to the question posed. The mooter then weaves the Waldo into the conclusion of his answer by reminding the court that what is at stake is the victim's "meaningful judicial process." In doing so, the panel is reminded of the core interest, right, duty, or obligation that is at stake.[11]

Thus far, we have characterized a moot as a persuasive, structured conversation. True to form, mooters should aim to be "**off-book**" when delivering their submissions. This is another best practice that mooters can employ to enhance the delivery of their submissions.

By "off book" we do not recommend rote memorization. Memorizing submissions is *not* effective. It is very distracting to the bench. Judges may be more fascinated with the actual feat of memorization rather than with the substantive arguments. Moreover, it is a human tendency when reciting a script from memory to blurt out the memorized text in an abrupt, hurried, and monotone fashion. This does not send a message of knowledge, skill, or confidence and will negatively impact one's overall moot score.

Being off-book means that the script should serve as an aid to remind the mooter of her essential points. A mooter should never be married to the text of the script or factum. Being off-book allows the student to maintain eye contact with all members of a judicial bench. Eye contact is one of the factors measured on most moots (either explicitly or subconsciously). Eye contact makes the judge feel important, as though the mooter is addressing him specifically. Eye contact is also commonly seen as a sign of confidence and sincerity. A mooter's

---

8 Harvard Law School, *Introduction to Advocacy, Research, Writing, and Argument*, 7th ed. by David Ware, Gregory Lantier, & Mandana Dashtaki (New York: Foundation Press, 2002) at 71.

9 We adopt this word from the lectures of the Honourable Justice Abbey, a special lecturer in Civil Procedure at the University of Windsor, Faculty of Law. The Waldo is a mooter's core position or core narrative. It is often repeated during a mooter's submissions in order to subtly reinforce the underlying theme or "big picture." In effect, it serves to prevent the panel from asking, "Where's Waldo?"

10 *United States of America v. Ferras; United States of America v. Latty*, 2006 SCC 33 at para. 19.

11 The Honourable Justice John I. Laskin, "What Persuades (or, What's Going on Inside the Judge's Mind)" (Summer 2004) 23:1 Advocates' Soc. J. Justice Laskin summed it up mathematically: Persuasive Burden = Distance × Resistance. A mooter's persuasive burden is lessened if they can reduce the panel's resistance. Waldos help to remind the panel of the underlying "justice" that is being sought. Perhaps Justice Laskin's equation could be rewritten as follows: Persuasive Burden = Distance × Resistance (divided by Waldos).

submissions will be more believable and engaging. More importantly, maintaining eye contact allows an advocate to effectively read the bench.

Identifying the body language and demeanour of the panel enables a mooter to make strategic adjustments in delivery. For example, a panellist appearing confused or interested may reflect this state with raised eyebrows or a lean forward. This behaviour can only be discerned by looking at the panel. A good mooter should pick up these non-verbal cues and react accordingly. For example, a mooter might slow her delivery and make a bit more eye contact with this panellist as to indicate a willingness to be questioned, or slow down to permit the panellist to better assimilate what is being said. Being able to read a bench in this way is often what separates a good performance from a superb performance.

Finally, an off-book mooter is better able to demonstrate a mastery of his submissions. Judges in a moot court are often deliberately attempting to divert students away from their script. Mooters who are already off-book will maintain the same demeanour and composure when questioned (even by irrelevant lines of questioning). It is this seamless delivery that should be aimed for. Being off-book enables a smooth, effortless transition in and out of submissions. The ability to seamlessly return to one's submissions after being side-tracked is the hallmark of an excellent mooter

These are the basics of an effective oral argument. In the following chapter we discuss common phraseology in mooting and then we turn our attention to dealing with questions from the bench in Chapter 6.

CHAPTER 5

Terminology and Phrases

Language shapes our perceptions, and the language of mooting is no exception. Well-chosen words and phrases play a pivotal role in the art of persuasion.[1] Of primary importance is the manner in which the bench is addressed. The Supreme Court of Canada has issued practice directions that clearly outline the rules regarding this:

> At the hearing, counsel may use either "Justice," "Mr. Justice," or "Madam Justice," when addressing the members of the panel hearing the appeal. Counsels are asked to refrain from addressing the judges as "My Lord," "My Lady," "Your Lordship," or "Your Ladyship."[2]

And since moot competitions are intended to represent the "supreme" appellate level or "supreme" moot court, we suggest that moot participants abide by the above practice directions. Haughty terms like "My Lord," "My Lady," "Your Lordship," "Your Ladyship," "Your Excellency," and iterations thereof, should

---

[1] One study on persuasion found that words factored 53 percent, while body language and tone are 32 and 15 percent respectively. See, Harry Mills, *Artful Persuasion* (New York: AMA Publications, 2000) at 41–43.

[2] The Supreme Court of Canada, "Frequently Asked Questions," online: The Supreme Court of Canada www.scc-csc.gc.ca/faq/faq/index-eng.asp#f10. The Federal Court (Canada) (which has hosted the Harold G. Fox Moot Intellectual Property Moot, the Corporate/Securities Moot and the Bertha Wilson Moot) has also issued similar directions. See, Federal Court (Canada), "Frequently Asked Questions," online: Federal Court (Canada) cas-ncr-nter03.cas-satj.gc.ca/portal/page/portal/fc_cf_en/FAQ#20. These terms also carry certain sexist and religionist baggage that may account for their abandonment as well.

never be used.[3] "Your Honour" may be used, but the preferred salutation is "Mr. Justice" or "Madam Justice."

A mooter may also address a member of the panel by his or her surname, which creates an air of preparation and formality; for example, "Mr. Justice Hutchinson" or "Madam Justice Carasco." However, this is optional and should only be done where the last name is easily pronounceable (and easily memorized). The bench would hardly be impressed if a mooter mixed up the names of the panellists (especially if the panellists consist of widely known members of the judiciary[4]). The safest approach is simply "Mr. Justice" or "Madam Justice." When referring to the Chief Justice[5] (whether fictional or not), it is best to adopt a gender-neutral title—"Chief Justice McLachlin" or "Chief Justice Lutfy."[6] Avoid use of "Madame Chief Justice" or "Mr. Chief Justice."

In addition to addressing judges, there are practice rules that should be adopted when referring to other parties as well. For instance, when referring to one's own case, mooters should not personalize their delivery.[7] Phrases such as "I think," "I feel," [8] "in my opinion," or "we believe" should all be avoided as they are informal and misleading. A mooter is not advancing a personal position (therefore, they do not "think," "feel," or "believe"), they are advancing a submission for their client's position.

Opposing counsel should be referred to as "my friend" or "my friends."[9] This tradition stems from the recognition that counsel should treat each other with respect[10] (and from the historical fact that most counsel were "friends" having been trained at, or belonging to, a small number of Inns or Law Schools). The term "my learned friend" is usually reserved for Queen's Counsels, or in jurisdictions like Ontario and Quebec where the Q.C. designation has fallen

---

3 We should note that "My Lord" and "My Lady" (and iterations thereof) are still used by many Provincial Superior Courts. However, the practice directions issued by the Federal Court (Canada) and the Supreme Court of Canada are progressive and sensible.

4 For instance, we have seen student mooters refer to the Chief Justice of the Federal Court (Canada) as "Justice Lufty."

5 The Chief Justice of the panel is the panellist who sits in the middle of a panel of three, five, seven, or even nine panellists. If the panel has an even number of panellists, the Chief Justice will be pointed out to mooters.

6 Careful readers will note the correct spelling of the Chief Justice Lutfy's surname.

7 Alan D. Hornstein, *Appellate Advocacy in a Nutshell*, 2d ed. (St. Paul, MN: West Group, 1998) at 250.

8 There has been some suggestion that these restrictions reflect a sexist bias in advocacy. Namely, advocates should be emotionless (an advocate does not feel); they are simply autonomous agents for their clients. There might be some merit to these views, but we are not rewriting the rules of the game in this book—we are merely setting them out.

9 Phrases like "my worthy opponent" are reserved for high school and undergraduate debates, not competitive moots. It is usually a sign of poor training if mooters refer to opposing counsel as their "worthy opponents."

10 Etiquette will be discussed further in Chapter 7.

into disuse, to refer to very senior members of the Bar. Student mooters, by definition, would never qualify as "learned friends" and should avoid use of the phrase (despite how flattering it may be).

Abbreviations should also be avoided when delivering oral submissions. Abbreviations, even if used in the factum, do not have the same effect during oral argument. Consider even the most common abbreviation, "S.C.C." Even if it takes the panellist a few seconds to mentally expand the abbreviation, these are precious seconds that are diverted from a mooter's submissions. Furthermore, whenever a mooter is invoking an S.C.C. decision, it is worth emphasizing the entire term due to the sheer weight of these decisions. Between saying, "the S.C.C. has held that patents over higher life-forms . . ." or "the Supreme Court of Canada has held that patents over higher life-forms . . ." it is the latter that impresses upon the Court the authority and decisiveness of the decision.

The issue of abbreviations will also arise when dealing with cases with lengthy names. The Supreme Court of Canada decision in *Society of Composers, Authors and Music Publishers of Canada v. Canadian Assn. of Internet Providers*[11] is a good illustration. Repeating this decision more than once takes at least 10 seconds (assuming one doesn't jumble the words). To ensure that time is not wasted labouring over lengthy case names, a mooter, when introducing the name of the case for the first time, should read the entire case title and then follow it with the abbreviation that will be used from that point on. The aforementioned case would be abbreviated as "SOCAM."

Analogies should also be avoided during oral submissions. An analogy may seem clever, but it is dangerous in moots. Understandably, mooters use analogies to demonstrate complicated principles. Student mooters feel that this demonstrates a command of the legal principle involved and its application to an analogous set of facts. However, analogies backfire. This is especially true of a seemingly clever and well-constructed analogy, which inevitably invites rebuttals and questioning from the panel.[12] Worse yet, panellists seem to delight in "poking holes" in analogies, or proposing a counter-analogy.

For instance, in a labour law moot, we have seen a mooter (representing the employer) argue that post-termination confidentiality clauses are the "snow tires in the vehicle of an employment contract." This was immediately followed by a quip from a panellist that the contract would be quite inefficient and ineffectual during the fall, spring, and summer months. The student then attempted to explain that the confidentiality clause was merely a safety mechanism to remind former employees of their post-termination confidentiality obligations.

---

11 2004 SCC 45.

12 There are some simple analogies that are acceptable however. For instance, the likening of the constitution to a "living tree" is a common example. We do not consider these to be "true" analogies since they were not created by the mooter. They are better characterized as legal clichés.

This irritated the panel even more. Another panellist "reminded" the student that the common law already imposes confidentiality obligations on employees post-termination, and any unconscionable post-termination obligations that the employer tried to enforce on the employee through contract would not be upheld. "The 'common law' is the road salt and snow removal equipment; your client does not need winter tires in a large city," bellowed the panellist. The analogy was defeated, and the mooter's position (and confidence) was visibly lost amongst the crossfire.

Other than analogies, there are also certain phrases to avoid when participating in a moot. Justice Finlayson has set out a series of phrases which judges tend to frown upon.[13] The phrases most relevant to mooting are:

- I did not prepare my factum.
- That isn't in my friend's factum.
- I did not understand my friend to have said that.
- My friend would have the court believe . . .
- The trial judge did not deal with that.
- I will be coming to that later in my argument.
- My colleague will address that point.[14]

As for the last phrase, there *may* be times when a mooter's colleague will indeed address that point. However, this is not an excuse to slough questions onto a mooter's co-counsel (who themselves may be scrambling to recall the precise question). In fact, this is an ideal opportunity for the mooter to state, "although my co-counsel will be addressing this in their submissions, perhaps I can briefly address it here . . . ." The bench will be impressed by the mere fact that the mooter addressed the question "head on," even though it was not within the ambit of her submissions.

In addition to Justice Finlayson's list, students should also be mindful of the phrase "it is respectfully submitted." When preparing a factum, this phrase is often used as a matter of formality. However, as noted above, oral submissions are not a recitation of one's factum. In other words, it is safe to assume that everything spoken is "respectfully submitted." Furthermore, a mooter should avoid lifting "artificial" phrases directly from their factum. A moot is a structured conversation. No one says "it is respectfully submitted" in a conversation, even when speaking to a judge.

Students are often coached to state "if it pleases the Court, I will now turn to my third point" when transitioning from one submission to another. This phrase instinctively prompts a question from the bench, especially where the

---

13 The Honourable George Finlayson, "Appellate Advocacy in an Abbreviated Setting" (1999) 18:2 Advocates' Soc. J. 22.
14 *Ibid.* at 25.

Court was not pleased with a mooter's earlier submission. It unconsciously signals to the bench that a mooter is leaving this submission and does not plan on returning to it. It is more effective for a mooter to use phrases such as "with that said, I want to turn the Court's attention to . . ." or "having said that, I turn now to my second point in issue." These phrases are more subtle. Moreover, these phrases do not arrogantly assume that the Court is entirely convinced (or "pleased") with a mooter's previous submissions.

CHAPTER 6

Dealing with Questions

"In law . . . the right answer usually depends on putting the right question."[1]
—The Honourable Justice Frankfurter

The most dynamic part of a moot is the interaction between the bench of judges and the oralist in front of them. Questions from the bench represent the best opportunity to separate good mooters from the outstanding ones. It is also one of the primary criteria that judges use to determine the top teams and top mooters in the competition. Top mooters have an ability to maintain their composure and respond intelligently and confidently to questions from the bench. This skill comes with practice, but some basic principles are helpful.

There are two types of benches in a moot—hot and cold. A skilled mooter knows how to deal with both types. As Carol Berry writes:

> Panels that are well-equipped with the intricacies of the case will often ask many questions. A characteristic of these panels is their willingness to interrupt the mooter mid-sentence, and even during their opening remarks. A mooter's time is usually monopolized in answering questions from the bench. This type of panel is referred to as a **Hot Bench**.
>
> A **Cold Bench**, on the other hand, is more concerned with the submissions of the mooter. (A Cold Bench may also simply be out of their depths with respect to the subject matter, or neglected to read the factums ahead of time). These

---

[1]   Per the Honourable Justice Frankfurter in *Rogers v. Commissioner of Internal Revenue*, 320 U.S. 410 at 413 (1943).

benches will rarely interrupt a mooter. Questions from a Cold Bench tend to focus on the facts of the case.[2]

Obviously, an advocate must prepare for either scenario. Submissions must be mastered to deal with either hot or cold benches. Students who are able to identify the type of panel in advance will be able to make adjustments to their delivery and increase its persuasiveness. Some panellists in moot competitions have developed a reputation for being "hot" or "cold." Out of respect we will not mention them here, but seasoned mooters are aware of them. Also, this is where the respondent may have an edge, since they present their submissions after the appellant and can get a better sense of the panel's "heat."

Mooters should practice their submissions using the **60/40 Rule**. A mooter should allot sixty percent of their time to their submissions and expect that the remaining forty percent will be occupied with questions. In a twenty minute moot, submissions should be tailored to occupy twelve minutes of that time, with the remaining eight minutes allotted for questions from the bench.

For a Hot Bench the 60/40 Rule is inverted. Mooters should expect that sixty percent of their time will be occupied with questions from the bench, with the other forty percent devoted to submissions. A mooter's concluding remarks, and later submissions, will have to be shortened.

For a Cold Bench we split the difference. That is, a Cold Bench will usually monopolize about twenty percent of a mooter's time with questions. Mooters can either slow the pace of their delivery, or simply end their submissions early. There is no rule that requires an oralist to use all of his or her allotted time. If a mooter has made her submissions and answered the questions from the bench, and there is time remaining, then sit down. Do not become friendly or quizzical inviting more questions—simply conclude and sit down.[3]

Now, some tips in answering questions from the bench.

Do not dread questions from the bench. This is the point of oral (as opposed to written) advocacy. And, although questions from the bench should be welcomed, a mooter should never thank the panellist for the question, nor should the mooter compliment the judge on an "excellent question." It is the job of the bench to ask questions. All of their questions are excellent.

Judges will often ask questions during a mooter's submissions because the oralist has mounted an effective argument and the panel wishes to test it. Other times, a panellist simply wishes to throw a mooter "off-track." Regardless of

---

2   Carole C. Berry, *Effective Appellate Advocacy: Brief Writing and Oral Argument*, 7th ed. (St. Paul, MN: West Group, 1999) at 145.

3   At the 2007–2008 Bertha Wilson Moot we observed a mooter employ this tactic with great success. The panel was so impressed with the mooter's overall submissions that they remarked that the case had "already been won," and the respondent need not take the podium. The mooter was eventually named second top oralist for the entire moot.

the panel's motives, a mooter must always show deference to the panel. When interrupted by a judge, a mooter must stop talking immediately and give the panellist their undivided attention.[4] This not only demonstrates a high level of respect, it allows the mooter to strategically absorb the question without distraction. Mooters must "listen before they leap."[5]

The general tendency of mooters to deliver "pre-recorded" answers is not recommended. In preparing for the moot, students will often anticipate certain questions and rehearse answers for them. This practice is extremely detrimental to success at competitive moots for two main reasons.

First, a question from the bench represents an opportunity to engage in dialogue with the bench. Delivering a scripted response to a question stifles this dialogue, as panellists can easily detect a pre-recorded answer. Judges may not feel engaged or appreciated, and the panel may quickly become cold.

Second, pre-recorded responses are often not what the panellist is looking for, in terms of a response. Indeed, students are often misguided by a false sense of security that pre-recorded responses give. In reality, the mooter has squandered an opportunity to engage in dialogue with the bench.

This should not be construed as a blanket ban on anticipating questions. Questions that are anticipated during practice will usually be the same general "type" of questions that the panel will ask.[6] However, a pre-recorded response should always be tailored and reformulated to address a panellist's specific question. Mooters must take a moment, understand and absorb the question, and *tailor* their rehearsed response accordingly.

With this broad understanding of judicial questioning, we now proceed to a more rigorous examination. In addition to anticipating the substantive questions from a panel, students should familiarize themselves with the types of questions they are likely to encounter during the course of a moot. Justice Binnie, of the Supreme Court of Canada, has identified seven types of questions that an advocate can expect to see at the appellate level:[7]

(1) Enlightenment questions;
(2) Confrontational questions;
(3) Reformulation questions;
(4) Hostile-fire questions;
(5) Collateral-fire questions

---

4   John Searles, *Advocacy in the Moot Court Program: An Analysis of the Fundamentals of Legal Research, Brief Writing and Oral Advocacy for the Beginning Appellate Advocate*, 3d ed. (Cincinnati: The W.H. Anderson Company, 1971) at 20.

5   The Honourable Justice Ian Binnie, "A Survivor's Guide to Advocacy in the Supreme Court of Canada" (1999) 18:2 Advocates' Soc. J. 13 at 18.

6   Master Donkin (Ret.), "Parting Shots from the Master's Bench" (1999) 18:1 Advocates' Soc. J. 18.

7   Binnie, above note 5 at 18–19.

(6) Cross-fire questions; and

(7) "Martland" questions.

Each of these questions requires a brief description and comment on how to deal with them.

1. **Enlightenment questions** are questions of general inquiry. A judge simply wishes to understand the case better. These are usually broad questions about the facts or the particular statute (or collection of case law) applicable to the case. This type of questioning can be easily anticipated and prepared for in advance.

2. **Confrontational questions** are questions based on the position of opposing counsel. These questions take the general form of: "Counsel your friend has said that this case focuses on your client's duty to mitigate, can you elaborate on this?" In a moot, these questions are easy to anticipate since students will have practiced with the appellant pair or respondent pair from their own school in preparing for the moot or received the factum of their opponent in advance of the moot (as is common practice with nearly all moots).

3. **Reformulation questions** are rare gems in moot court. A judge will summarize the submission being advanced and ask if she is correct in her summation. These questions are to be cherished, as they represent an opportunity to agree with the judge and affirm the understanding in a polite, laudatory manner. If, however, the reformulation is not accurate, a mooter should soften the blow by responding with a subtle negative, such as "not entirely Madame Justice, perhaps my point is better seen when dealing with my second submission." This provides the mooter with an opportunity to continue with his submissions, while still acknowledging the bench.

4. **Hostile-fire questions** are exactly what the name implies. In this scenario, the panellist usually expresses (mild) disgust with the argument being advanced. We have seen panellists ask, "Counsel are you *actually* saying that all jokes are defamatory? Really?" These questions must be approached with a calm poise. A judge has effectively emphasized—albeit inaccurately—the issue and argument raised by the mooter. Responses should demonstrate poise with a simple reframing of the submission. To continue with the above example, the mooter could respond, "Certainly not Madame Justice, what I am saying, however, is that there are some crude jokes that, given their context, have the clear potential to be defamatory." (In most defamation actions, context is especially relevant, and so the mooter deflects the hostile-fire question and places this Waldo into her answer. Win-win.)

5. **Collateral-fire questions** are questions from the bench that direct a mooter to another submission or different point of law. For example, a judge may state, "Counsel, I am more interested in your third point on minimal impairment." These questions must be answered immediately. The natural in-

clination is to politely remark that the third point will be discussed later in submissions, but this is not effective. "Later" may not occur (especially with a Hot Bench), and such a response squanders an opportunity for the mooter to address something that is currently on the judge's mind.[8] It is also an ideal moment for the mooter to demonstrate his skill in moving between submissions and going off-book. A collateral-fire question is an opportunity to score marks. Simple.

6. **Cross-fire questions** are rare in moots. These are a series of questions (and answers) between the mooter and members of the panel — either from the same panellist or the entire bench. A panellist will ask a confrontational-reformulation question, and force the mooter to adopt the hostile reformulation. A second panellist (or the same panellist) will then interject with her own hostile reformulation in rapid succession. In these instances a student should avoid adopting any reformulation; instead, he should rephrase the hostile reformulation in a way that aligns to his original submission. A mooter that valiantly but respectfully holds his ground will (eventually) garner the respect of the bench. This leads to an important point: do not take questions personally. No bench is trying to personally attack a mooter, no matter how hostile the questions may seem.

7. Last is the **"Martland" question** (as categorized by Justice Binnie). These questions are queries that a mooter has not anticipated and may not have an answer for. Justice Binnie describes these questions as:

> The seventh and last category of question is what used to be called the "Martland question." Justice Martland, during the 1970s and early '80s, was not inclined to ask many questions, but he would sit and fret and fool around with his papers and look quizzical and scratch an ear and call for books to be sent in, and talk to his neighbours, but at some point in the proceeding there would be a kind of chilly silence and Martland would clear his throat and out would come the question, trailing wisps of smoke behind it. There wasn't anybody in the courtroom who didn't realize that the moment of truth had arrived. If you were able to deal with the Martland question the case was as good as won, and you felt yourself galloping toward the sunlit uplands of victory. If you failed, a kind of a death watch set in.[9]

While Justice Binnie may have painted a dim picture for members of the practising bar, the same may not be true for mooters. Remember, mooters are law students. Some amount of failure is tolerated by the moot judges. The easiest way to deal with a "Martland" question is to simply rephrase it in a way that

---

8   New York University Law School, *Moot Court Handbook: Introduction to Brief Writing and Oral Argument*, 2d ed. (New York: New York School of Law, 1968) at 73.

9   Binnie, above note 5 at 19.

makes it answerable. This skill requires the precision of a surgeon's knife, and the confidence of a politician. We have seen it done a few times—and like Justice Binnie's observation—if the bench accepted the rephrasing of the question, the mooter inevitably galloped towards success. In cases where the bench did not accept the rephrasing, the questioning became more heated and the mooter's entire submissions usually unravelled.[10]

Now that we have covered the various types of benches and types of questions, mooters should also know that the ideal answer to any question will contain both fact and law in the response.[11]

First the response must be grounded in some factual context. Preparing a fact sheet in addition to scripted submissions is essential.[12] This sheet should clearly and efficiently set out the primary facts of the case; and the location of those facts within the judgment and the factum.[13]

Armed with the fact sheet, a mooter should respond to questions from the bench with a factual foundation that is supplemented with a legal argument—preferably case law. This strategy demonstrates a mastery of the case as well as the jurisprudence. Most mooters simply recite the case law in their response. While this is not wrong in an academic sense, it sends a negative message to the panel. If the response to a question is an abrupt recitation of case law, the mooter has implicitly devalued the question. Mooters should never devalue (or dismiss) a question from the bench.

Some responses however, may not satisfy a panel and follow-up questions are often asked. As a general rule, students should have two back-up responses to questions before shifting focus or conceding the point. Concessions must be done in a tactful manner so as to demonstrate a willingness to be flexible in argument, but not to signal overall weakness. Mooters should avoid the word "concede" as it sends a message to the panel that a particular point is very weak.[14] Ideally, a mooter could accept the bench's comment with a simple, "I take your point Madame Justice." This is a subtle yet effective concession. It can then be followed by a shift in focus to a stronger submission.

Another tactic when conceding a point is to state, "Why yes Mr. Justice, as you have pointed out, I would have to agree with my friend's assertion, but, in

---

10 Or, in keeping with our galloping horse analogy, the mooter simply came unglued.

11 Harvard Law School, *Introduction to Advocacy, Writing, and Argument*, 7th ed. by David Ware, Gregory Lantier, & Mandana Dashtaki (New York: Foundation Press, 2002) at 78.

12 The Honourable Justice Renee M. Pomerance, "Appellate Advocacy: Presenting the Oral Argument" (May 2002) online: The Supreme Court Advocacy Institute www.scai-ipcs/ca/pdf/ Pomerance-PresentingtheOralArgument.pdf.

13 As an example, see Appendix B.

14 Indeed, a concession may be interpreted quite broadly by a panellist. In the 2007 BLG Labour Arbitration Moot we observed a mooter who unwittingly conceded a point during questioning, only to have the judge ask if the student had effectively conceded the entire case.

my submission, this case does not turn on that particular issue, it turns, Justices, on my third point." This tactic provides for a seamless transition back to the mooter's original, scripted submissions, while subtly conceding a difficult or tricky point.

There is another skill that is useful for serious, competitive mooters: know your bench. We have hinted at this already in our discussion on hot and cold benches. But here we mean actually know *who* the members on your bench are — especially if they are (or were) prominent litigators or have written seminal judgments in this area of law. For instance, Mr. Justice Hughes was a panellist on the Final Bench of the 2008–2009 Harold G. Fox Intellectual Property Moot. He asked one of the finalists, "Didn't the Supreme Court in *Compo v. Blue Crest* say something about copyright law being statutory in nature or something?" Had the finalist *truly* been aware of the case law in this area, he would have immediately realized that the Supreme Court of Canada in *Compo Co. Ltd. v. Blue Crest Music et al.*[15] actually cited Justice Hughes in his days as a famous intellectual property litigator:

> Mr. Hughes for the respondent in answer to a question from the Bench put it very well when he said that copyright law is neither tort law nor property law in classification, but is statutory law. It neither cuts across existing rights in property or conduct nor falls between rights and obligations heretofore existing in the common law.[16]

It was an ideal opportunity for the mooter to demonstrate their true mastery of the jurisprudence.

15 [1980] 1 S.C.R. 357.
16 *Ibid.* at 372.

CHAPTER 7

Other Matters

No book on mooting would be complete without some words on etiquette. Etiquette is intimately connected to an oralist's overall presence at the podium. We have already indicated that mooters should refer to their opponents as "friends" during their submissions; personal, snide, or caustic remarks should also be avoided.[1]

So too, have we already stressed the importance of inflection. However, inflection should serve to emphasize a point by slightly raising one's tone or pitch—but never by yelling. Mooters should always speak at an audible volume, but at no point should they ever escalate to outright yelling. Students unconsciously use an elevated tone when disagreeing with a point or question from the panel, and they should note that, "Counsel can disagree, even vigorously, without being disagreeable."[2] A mooter must remember to respectfully disagree with the point, and not the person.

Eye contact is another element of etiquette. We have already discussed this in terms of sincerity. Eye contact denotes sincerity (or lack of deceit). However, there are other aspects of eye contact. Mooters often engage in **"tunnel vision"** whereby the mooter focuses on one member of the panel. The mooter will either focus on the Chief Justice (because of the perceived importance of the Chief Justice on the bench), the most active member of the panel, or the panellist who nods and smiles at the mooter (as these are unconscious cues that the panellist

---

1   Robert White Q.C. & The Honourable Justice Joseph Stratton, *The Appeal Book* (Aurora, ON: Canada Law Book, 1999) at 164.

2   Advocates' Society, *The Principles of Civility*, online: www.forces.gc.ca/jag/publications/directives/Directive006-00-B-eng.pdf at 4.

is in agreement with the mooter's submissions). This tunnel vision alienates the other members of the bench. All judges need to "feel the love." Justice Binnie correctly advises that good advocates are the ones who "[play] to every corner of the auditorium."[3] A mooter should maintain an equal amount of eye contact with all members of the panel, regardless of who is the Chief Justice, who might be the most active, or who is the most agreeable.

The next matter is humour. The use of humour in oral submissions is an extremely delicate art. Justice Sopinka outlines the inherent dilemma facing advocates:

> A little humour often provides welcome relief for the court. Not everyone can get away with it. With some counsel it appears strained and unnatural. Even those to whom it comes naturally must be careful in picking the right moment. There are times when the court is not in the right frame of mind for humour.[4]

Indeed, few lawyers are able to read the entire bench with some degree of accuracy. A student mooter would fare no better, and should never be humorous with their bench. Never. A bench that is on a mooter's "side" might be dismayed by the mooter's lack of respect in using inappropriately-timed humour.

The attentive reader will note that many of the judges we have cited throughout this book have written their articles or delivered their speeches with a great deal of humour. This is not unintentional. Lawyers have delicate egos, especially litigators. Humour is an extremely effective mechanism for delivering an otherwise important message about advocacy, professionalism, and etiquette; especially where the deliverer of that message is a respected and established member of the judiciary. Mooters have not attained this level of "goodwill." Mooters are students, and are often viewed as young, naïve, and impetuous. The theatrics of mooting do not call for humour on the part of the student. If the bench wishes to be humorous, then this is their prerogative. But a student should never respond "in kind" to a humorous bench. A student should remain respectful at all times.[5]

Timing is another matter that needs to be addressed. We have already mentioned the 60/40 Rule in timing one's submissions, but there are other matters

---

3   The Honourable Justice Ian Binnie, "A Survivor's Guide to Advocacy in the Supreme Court of Canada" (1999) 18:2 Advocates' Soc. J 13 at 13.

4   The Honourable Justice John Sopinka & Mark Gelowitz, *The Conduct of an Appeal*, 2d ed. (Markham, ON: Butterworths, 2000) at 286.

5   We have seen a moot where a judge of the Ontario Court of Appeal remarked that "Justice Binnie is a good friend of mine, are you disagreeing with him? And by the way, Justice Bastarache is also a good friend." Amongst the widespread laughter that emanated from spectators by that comment, the mooter quipped, "I am not impugning your social agenda, your honour." The attentive mooter would have noted that the other two panellists (both experienced judges as well) were not amused in the least.

that need to be mentioned, as time management is crucial to success at any moot.

First of all, pacing. People speak on average of 120 to 180 words a minute.[6] However, when pressured with time constraints (or nerves), there is an innate human tendency to accelerate this speed. A mooter must learn to control these tendencies, as speaking too quickly may cause disinterest or confusion among panellists. Mooters should never increase their speed when confronted with time constraints, heated questions, or sheer nerves. However, sometimes mooters may need to decrease their ordinarily acceptable pace to permit the bench to make notes. Eye contact, again, is essential in reading the bench. If panellists are writing something, this is usually a good thing. Slow down. The panel will miss fewer of a mooter's submissions once they've stopped writing.

Next, students must honour the clock.[7] In moot competitions, timekeepers use time cards (or other indicators) at certain intervals to indicate the time remaining. For instance, if a mooter has twenty minutes of allotted time, there will be indications that the mooter has ten, five, or two minutes remaining. Then there is usually a final card or indicator signalling that time is up.

Subject to the 60/40 Rule, a mooter should generally know where they ought to be at a particular point. For instance, most moots usually have an indicator around the halfway mark, and again when there are five minutes remaining. During practice rounds, mooters should know where they want to be in their submissions. (Indeed, there is no rule that each submission must be given equal time. Sometimes a submission has levels of detail that need to be explored in depth; whereas other submissions may require less explanation.)

At the two-minute mark (or the one-minute mark, depending on the competition), the mooter should not launch into her next submission. This is not the time to hurry through the remainder of one's submissions. Instead, the student should move to her concluding remarks, with the following statement: "Justices, I see that my time is nearing an end. I direct you to my factum for my [third] submission and would like to use the time remaining to make the following points in conclusion." In instances where time expires midway in a sentence, students should finish that sentence only.[8] If the point being conveyed is still incomplete, a student may ask the court for a brief extension in time. This extension is not a right and a bench will only allow these extensions with a view to them being brief. If granted, an extension should never exceed one minute.

An effective closing remark is one that is short and to the point. It reintroduces a mooter's Waldo, followed by one to two sentences to support the accuracy

---

6   Harry Mills, *Artful Persuasion* (New York: AMA Publications, 2000) at 89.

7   B. Bucholtz, M. Frey, & M. Tatum, *The Little Black Book: A Do-It Yourself Guide for Law Student Competitions* (Durham, NC: Carolina Academic Press, 2002) at 75.

8   Also a "sentence" is usually a few words. Your sentence should not drag into an entire paragraph. Don't get "cute."

of this core theory. Afterward, it closes with an order sought (similar to the one made in the opening remark). And, as a matter of custom, a mooter should close his submissions with the following text: "Subject to any further questions, these are my submissions. May I be of any further assistance to the Court?"[9] A polite nod is then exchanged with the bench, and the mooter takes his seat.

The final matter we will address is the **right of reply**—the Siren's song of mooting. The right of reply is an optional allotment of time (usually between two and five minutes) that is given to the appellant (or first team) to rebut what has just been said by their opponents. Therefore, the right of reply is a "reply" to the respondent's (or second team's) submissions. Justice Finlayson has characterized it as follows:

> Last, but by no means least, I come to what is potentially the most effective, but regrettably the most misused, tool of advocacy: the reply. This is counsel's opportunity to get in the last word, and unfortunately, in too many cases, that last word does not always assist. Your first consideration is: should I say anything? Believe me when I tell you that saying nothing is never a mistake. Silence may not advance your case, but it most assuredly will not hurt it.[10]

There are two schools of thought about the right of reply.[11] The first holds that exercising the right of reply (in a moot) is useless. A judge in a moot court is not actually adjudicating the case and there is no need to retake the podium to attempt to win the case on its merits. According to this school, the right of reply may actually detract from one's earlier performance since it gives the bench one last opportunity to take a few more "digs." Indeed, mooters should also be reminded that moot judges (like real judges, we presume) are human. Panellists have been hearing arguments for at least an hour. They might be grumpy. Exercising the right of reply—and exercising it badly—simply aggravates an already exhausted bench. Many times (more often than not) we have seen students exercise the right of reply by restating their original submissions only to be reminded by the panel that they have already made these points. The mooter then clumsily attempts to fill the remaining time with material they conjure up at that moment. The bench either allows the mooter to continue with her weak reply in awkward silence, or interrupts with a battery of "Martland" questions.

The second school of thought urges students to exercise the right of reply. However, the right of reply should only be exercised if there is something "new" to reply to. The right of reply is not an opportunity to make a mooter's submis-

---

9 Most panellists understand that this is a custom in mooting. In fact, we have never seen a panel member say, "Yes, you can be of further assistance," and then launch into a question.

10 The Honourable Justice George Finlayson, "Appellate Advocacy in an Abbreviated Setting" (1999) 18:2 Advocates' Soc. J. 22 at 24.

11 Of the two authors, Mohamed R. Hashim subscribes to the first school of thought, and Emir Aly Crowne-Mohammed subscribes to the second.

sions, or make one's strongest submission, one last time. All too often students are taught to always exercise the right of reply as it represents one last "kick at the can." This leads to many poor and inappropriate replies. Mooters should use the following decision tree to decide whether or not to exercise the right of reply:

1. The quality of the submissions themselves:
   a. Has your friend raised new arguments not covered in your submissions?
   b. If so, were those "new" submissions damaging to your case, or otherwise central to the issue(s) to be decided?
2. The quality of the *delivery* of those submissions:
   a. Did you observe the bench during your friend's submissions? Did the bench seem to accept these "new" arguments?
   b. More importantly, did the bench seem more impressed with your friend's delivery as a whole?

Remember that moots are not really won on the merits of the case. In general, the right of reply should only be exercised if it helps a mooter's (or a team's) overall score. However, sometimes a mooter's initial submissions are so strong and impressive that *waiving* the right of reply merely bolsters this impression among the bench.[12] Keep this in mind.

---

12 In the 2008–2009 Corporate Securities Moot, we observed a mooter waive the right of reply by stating that, "the appellants are confident in our submissions Justices, and waive the right of reply," only to have bench encourage the mooter to actually retake the podium. The bench openly remarked, with a bit of a smile, that they wanted to hear *more* of what the appellant had to say. The mooter eventually took the third place oralist award in the entire moot.

CHAPTER 8

Conclusion

Competitive mooting is an extremely effective way for law students to learn substantive law, factum writing, teamwork, and advocacy. Properly structured and administered, competitive moots are the ideal way to introduce clinical and experiential aspects of the legal profession to students. Competitive mooting may not be "true" advocacy, but it is an exciting substitute for students that breaks from the dry, doctrinal nature of academia.

We predict that mooting will increase in popularity among law schools as a serious pedagogical tool. We encourage law schools to take a disciplined and structured approach to their mooting programs by providing formal classes on advocacy and engaging the coaching assistance of practitioners and members of the judiciary. As well, law schools should continue recognizing competitive moots as a "for credit" activity, as it takes a tremendous amount of preparation, dedication, and motivation to successfully compete in competitive moots. Faculty members who coach competitive moots should also receive credit for this supervision. Indeed, the reluctance of many faculty members to coach moot teams stems from this lack of "credit." We modestly propose that law schools offer a course release for every three moots supervised by a professor—this ensures that mooting remains a "for credit" activity for all involved.

We have endeavoured to set out many of the best practices for arguing motions and appellate level moots that we have gleaned as mooters, coaches, and moot organizers. We hope that your moot experiences are enjoyable and rewarding. And . . .

Subject to any further questions, these are our submissions.

Moot Problem from the 2009–2010 Harold G. Fox Intellectual Property Moot

HAROLD G. FOX MOOT

MOOT PROBLEM

October 16, 2009

1. The following are reasons and judgment of the Trial Court of Canada, Intellectual Property Division. The decision of the Trial Court was subsequently overturned by the Court of Appeal; the reasons and judgment for which are also set out below.
2. Both Courts have jurisdiction over all issues raised in their respective decisions. The standard of review adopted by the Court of Appeal is also correct and not the subject of appeal.
3. The decision of the Court of Appeal is now appealed to the Supreme Moot Court for Intellectual Property Appeals.
4. All of the issues raised in the reasons given by the lower courts should be addressed by counsel for Seedy Enterprises Ltd. or The Dead Bull Group Inc. in their submissions. Arguments not referenced in the reasons of the lower courts may be advanced by counsel in their submissions, but only if they relate to the issues identified in the lower courts' decisions. The subject matter of the appeal is confined to the law of patents, but reference to the *Food and Drugs Act* (and *Food and Drug Regulations*) is acceptable in addressing the issue(s).
5. The formalities of the remedy sought, and costs, are not to be addressed.

TRIAL COURT OF CANADA, INTELLECTUAL PROPERTY DIVISION

Date: 20090828
Docket: T-825-04
Citation: 2009 FCIP 150

Ottawa, Ontario, this 28th day of August, 2009

PRESENT: THE HONOURABLE MR. JUSTICE STRAYNED

BETWEEN:

SEEDY ENTERPRISES LTD.

Plaintiff

and

THE DEAD BULL GROUP INC.

Defendant

Heard at Ottawa, Ontario, on May 1–29, June 1–30, July 1–27.

Judgment delivered at Ottawa, Ontario, on August 28th, 2009.

REASONS FOR JUDGMENT

Strayned J.

[1] This action is an action brought by the plaintiff, Seedy Enterprises Ltd. for judgment under s. 60 of the *Patent Act*, R.S.C. 1985, c. P-4 (the "*Patent Act*" or the "*Act*") declaring Canadian Patent 6,456,007 (the '007 Patent) invalid and void.

[2] The '007 Patent is owned by the defendant, The Dead Bull Group Inc. ("Dead Bull"), and is entitled "Administration of a Tonic". The '007 Patent describes benefits to human beings who consume an extract made from grapefruit seeds in accordance with instructions provided in the patent. The '007 Patent teaches that the use of the extract will "increase alertness and mental acuity in the short term, despite pre-existing conditions of exhaustion or mental lassitude".

[3] For the reasons set out below, I find that the '007 Patent is invalid because the subject-matter claimed is not patentable as it is a method of medical treatment.

[4] Dead Bull is the well-known European originator of the Dead Bull caffeinated confection, "Corrida de Toros". Due to the raging success of Corrida de

Toros, and other Dead Bull brand products in the Canadian market, Dead Bull set up a research facility in Pamplemousse, Quebec.

[5] In the late 1980s, a researcher at the Dead Bull research lab, Dr. Manuel Rodríguez Sánchez, began to investigate the effect of grapefruit seed extract on rats. The rats demonstrated increased metabolism and physical activity. When placed in a laboratory maze the rats would scurry through it in a frenzied race. It was Dr. Sánchez who coined the popular term "rat race".

[6] Dr. Sánchez then began experimentation with human subjects in the 1990s. His results were, however, not as promising. This was largely due to Dead Bull's insistence that the grapefruit seed extract be added to Dead Bull's Corrida de Toros (as to produce a grapefruit version of the caffeinated confection). There was little quantifiable impact on metabolic (or muscle) activity when the combination drink was consumed. Undaunted, Dr. Sánchez diluted the grapefruit seed extract and administered this by itself (without being added to the Corrida de Toros) to a group of test subjects (primarily young professionals and students) in the late 1990s and similar effects were experienced by those subjects, to that of the rats. Various means of administration were tested and documented including oral doses, capsules, intravenous and other modes of entry into the human body.

[7] Thereafter, the researchers focussed most of their experimental work on isolating the effect(s) of the grapefruit seed extract. With little delay, Dr. Sánchez had determined that grapefruit seed extract in capsule form was the most efficient means of administering it. After more work, the advantages of taking two capsules at a spaced interval were observed.

[8] Dead Bull took action on two fronts. First, the company prepared and filed a Canadian patent application. Second, a Dead Bull Nutraceuticals division was created to market the grapefruit seed extract as a "nutraceutical". The product, entitled "Dry Grapefruit Juice" was introduced to a large and willing market of Canadian students and young professionals through a series of promotional events (like air races, ultimate curling championships and poker events), and was an immediate hit.

[9] The introduction of the Dry Grapefruit Juice nutraceutical product did not go unnoticed in the Canadian marketplace. Seedy Enterprises Ltd. ("Seedy") had been, for many years, a nutraceutical leader. Most of its sales were derived from its flax seed extract product which was purportedly effective in reducing tooth decay. Seedy's primary market was young adults and featured various slogans like "bringing flaxy back" and "flax don't floss". However, before attempting to enter the grapefruit seed extract niche, Seedy had discovered that Dead Bull's '007 Patent had issued. The '007 Patent was applied for in 2001 and issued in 2003.

[10] Seedy brought this action in 2004 to impeach the '007 Patent. As counsel for Seedy stated at trial, the purpose of the action is to allow Seedy to com-

pete with Dead Bull without fear of patent infringement.

[11] At the heart of this dispute is claim 1 of the '007 Patent. The entire claim reads:

> "The use of grapefruit seed extract for improving mental acuity in humans by ingesting 20 mg of said extract twice daily at an interval of between 20 and 30 minutes."

[12] The parties agree, as do their expert witnesses, that the subject-matter of this admirably brief claim is both novel and inventive. Before the work at Dead Bull's laboratory, nobody had appreciated that taking the grapefruit seed extract as set out in the patent would provide any benefit. Despite the use of grapefruit seed extract in other ways, the idea of using the grapefruit seed extract as taught in the patent would not have been obvious to a notional skilled worker at the time of publication of the patent.

[13] The parties, however, disagree as to whether the subject-matter of the claim is patentable under the *Act*. Section 2 of the *Patent Act* defines an "invention" as "any new and useful art, process, machine, manufacture or composition of matter, or any new and useful improvement in any art, process, machine, manufacture or composition of matter". However, not all 'inventions' satisfy this statutory definition. This impeachment proceeding, which effectively seeks a declaration of invalidity, requires me to determine whether the invention is patentable under Canadian law, or not.

[14] For the reasons set out below, I agree with Seedy that claim 1 is invalid as being directed towards non-patentable subject-matter.

[15] Claim 1 is defined as a "use" claim. There is no dispute that a new use for an old product may be patentable (*Shell Oil Co. v. Commissioner of Patents*, [1982] 2 S.C.R. 536). Thus, although grapefruit seed extract has been used for many years in various contexts, the fact that the patent claim recites the use of the extract for a new purpose is not, for that reason, objectionable.

[16] However, the use for the extract as set out in claim 1 is not for a commercial endeavour (such as lubrication of book spines (see Canadian Patent No. 5,000,001)), but is for a use that changes the physiological state of human beings. The patent's specification itself is unambiguous about this—"following the regimen of taking two 20 mg capsules approximately half an hour apart, subjects are brought from blurred mental states to sharper and more focussed states."

[17] Furthermore, as can be readily observed, although claim 1 refers to the "use" of the grapefruit seed extract, the claim is analogous to a *method* in that the claim defines a specific manner of taking the grapefruit seed extract.

[18] I agree with the capable argument of Seedy's counsel, Cunning Q.C., that claim 1 when considered in light of the '007 Patent as a whole, defines a method—a method of taking a particular substance to achieve a desired

physiological change in the person taking the substance. Thus, claim 1 covers a method of medical treatment. The grapefruit seed extract meets the criteria of a medicinal product, and the claim therefore defines a way that the medicinal product is to be taken by patients.

[19] Much was made in argument by Dead Bull as to the purported line between pharmaceutical and nutraceutical products. Although Canadian law does differentiate between pharmaceuticals and nutraceuticals in certain legal and regulatory contexts, I do not perceive there to be any distinction from the point of view of the *Patent Act*. There are many patentable products that are treated differently in law (and regulation) from each other. One would hardly expect a new children's toy and a terrorist's weapon to be subject to the same set of regulations and laws, yet from the perspective of patent law there is no basis for differentiating between the two.

[20] As the Canadian jurisprudence has defined a clear prohibition against the patentability of all methods of medical treatment (see, for example, *Tennessee Eastman Co. v. Commissioner of Patents*, [1974] S.C.R. 111), claim 1 of the '007 Patent is invalid. As all the other claims of the '007 Patent depend from claim 1, the patent is invalid in its entirety.

[21] Judgment and costs to the plaintiff accordingly.

COURT OF APPEAL

Date: 20091013
Docket: A-375-08
Citation: 2009 FCA 232

Ottawa, Ontario, this 13th day of October, 2009

CORAM: BILL J.A.,
          ABLE J.A.,
          HOURS J.A.

BETWEEN:

THE DEAD BULL GROUP INC.

Appellant

and

SEEDY ENTERPRISES LTD.

Respondent

Heard at Ottawa, Ontario, on October 1–6.

Judgment delivered at Ottawa, Ontario, on October 13th, 2009.

REASONS FOR JUDGMENT BY: ABLE J.A.

CONCURRED BY: HOURS J.A.
                BILL J.A.

REASONS FOR JUDGMENT

Able J.A.

[1] What is an invention? This is the 'subject-matter' of this appeal.

[2] The starting point for an appeal such as this is section 2 of the *Patent Act*, R.S.C. 1985, c. P-4 (the "*Patent Act*" or the "*Act*"). Section 2 defines an "invention" as:

> "any new and useful art, process, machine, manufacture or composition of matter, or any new and useful improvement in any art, process, machine, manufacture or composition of matter."

[3] At first instance, Strayned, J. held that claim 1 of Canadian Patent 6,456,007 (the '007 Patent) was not an "invention" under the *Act*. Although the

learned judge correctly identified that a new use for an old product is patentable under the *Act* (per *Shell Oil Co. v. Commissioner of Patents*, [1982] 2 S.C.R. 536), he misdirected himself as to the remainder of his inquiry. With all due respect, the decision below must be overturned.

[4] There are three issues that require consideration in analyzing the patentability of claim 1 of the '007 Patent:

1. Is the so-called "nutraceutical" product of the '007 Patent properly considered a "medicine"?; and if so,
2. Does claim 1 of the '007 Patent define a method?; and even if so,
3. Does the *Patent Act* preclude patentability for methods of medical treatment?

As set out below, this Court finds that each of these questions should be answered in the negative.

[5] I turn first to the question of whether the claimed benefits that come from taking the grapefruit seed extract as described in the patent are medicinal in nature. For the reasons set out below, I conclude that the claimed extract may provide certain benefits after consumption, but that this is insufficient to render the extract a medicine.

[6] Although the discovery of the extract's efficacy, by Dead Bull, was made in a scientific setting and was supported by clinical trials, this is not sufficient to render the subject-matter of the claims "medical". The fact that the product was marketed without the need for approval under the *Food and Drug Regulations* (C.R.C., c. 870) as a drug is further evidence to support a finding that the product is not a medicine. Under section 2 of the *Food and Drugs Act* (R.S., 1985, c. F-27) (the "*Food and Drugs Act*") a "drug" includes

"any substance or mixture of substances manufactured, sold or represented for use in

(a) the diagnosis, treatment, or mitigation of prevention of disease, disorder or abnormal physical state, or its symptoms, in human beings or animals,
(b) restoring, correcting or modifying organic functions in human beings or animals . . ."

Neither of these definitions of "drug" in the subsections is satisfied by the substance that is described in the '007 Patent (namely, the use of the grapefruit seed extract in combating fatigue). For this first reason, I reject the conclusion of Strayned, J. that the grapefruit seed extract is, in the context of the '007 Patent, a medicine. There is no pathological condition that is addressed by the solution described in the invention. The "symptoms" of being tired or unfocussed is endemic to the human condition and must be considered a symptom of being in a normal state, and not a pathological condition. If there is no pathology being addressed, there is no medicinal action occurring. I therefore disagree with the lower Court's finding.

[7] Second, claim 1 of the '007 Patent is not in the form of a "method" claim.

[8] The claim, as drafted, is to a *use* of the grapefruit seed extract, and not to a *method*. The role of the courts is to take a patent claim as drafted, and not re-write the claim based upon a judicial interpretation as to its "essence". By its very wording, the '007 Patent claims a new use and not a method.

[9] Therefore, the learned judge committed an error of law in finding that claim 1 was invalid as being directed to a method of medical treatment. The claim does not cover a method but rather a new use for an old product. Furthermore, even if the claim were otherwise held to be directed at a method and not a new use, as I have concluded above, the claim does not relate to a medicine (but rather to a nutraceutical product).

[10] Therefore, I find that claim 1 does not claim a method, nor does it relate to a medical use (or method). The so-called prohibition against patenting methods of medical treatment does not apply; and the invention is not excluded from patentability on that ground.

[11] In addition, even if (as the learned judge below concluded) claim 1 were directed at a method of medical treatment, I do not read the *Patent Act* as precluding the patentability of such a claim. Chief Justice McLachlin and Justice Fish, writing for the majority in *Monsanto Canada Inc. v. Schmeiser*, 2004 SCC 34 put it well at para. 94:

> "Our task, however, is to interpret and apply the *Patent Act* as it stands, in accordance with settled principles. Under the present *Act*, an invention in the domain of agriculture is as deserving of protection as an invention in the domain of mechanical science. Where Parliament has not seen fit to distinguish between inventions. . . neither should the courts."

[12] Therefore, since the current *Patent Act* does not itself contain any specific provision that bars the patentability of methods of medical treatment, it is not the role of the courts to re-write the *Act* or second guess Parliament's will. Accordingly, the decision in *Tennessee Eastman Co. v. Commissioner of Patents*, [1974] S.C.R. 111 must either be interpreted narrowly, or no longer considered good law.

[13] The extensive clinical trials carried out by Dead Bull, and the lengthy disclosure that is found in the '007 Patent, shows that this new use of the grapefruit seed extract has been extensively studied and is well-understood. There is clearly a benefit to the public in rewarding the work done by Dead Bull with the exclusive rights that a patent confers, in exchange for the public disclosure that the patent specification provides. The invention is patentable.

[14] For these reasons, I would allow the appeal.

"I agree."

Stephen Bill J.A.

"I too agree."
   Mary-Louise Hours J.A.

Sample Fact Sheet for Student Mooters

The following is a sample fact sheet a student may create for easy reference when responding to questions from the bench.

The facts are drawn from the 2008–2009 Davies, Ward, Phillip & Vineberg Corporate-Securities Moot.

Appellant	Respondent
Trial found:	*Facts*
• Unfair disregard (s. 241)	• Brewski ownership in Old Robdev was not viewed favourably by market analysts—regarded as a plaything (para. 8)
• And not fair and reasonable (s. 192)	
	• Because Old Robdev was a wholly owned subsidiary, only haphazard management took place (para. 8)
Facts	
• Legal control vests in De Beers 52% of the votes attaching to common shares (para. 6)	• The directors realized the negative impact of the Old Robdev and decided that if it was separated shareholder value could be enhanced (para. 9)
• Because it was a wholly owned subsidiary, only haphazard management took place (para. 8)	• Obtained legal and accounting advise from Brewski's professional advisors as to possible alternatives, the Board decided on a spin-off (para. 9)
• The spin-off was concluded to be most tax beneficial for both Brewski and its common shareholders (para. 9)	
• Based on the professional advice given to them, the Board decided that in order to carry out the spin-off on a tax deferral basis a butterfly transaction is acceptable (para. 10)	• The spin-off was concluded to be most tax beneficial for both Brewski and its common shareholders (para. 9)
• De Beers proposed the idea of a charitable foundation after the plan arrangement was agreed in principle and the Board agreed with unanimous approval (para. 12)	• De Beers withdrew from the Board meeting when the transaction was considered and did not vote as well—because he and his family had holdings in class B shares

Appellant	Respondent
• Pref. shares objected claiming pref. rights would be affected as it pertains to their rights on liquidation (para. 15) • Brewski gets legal advice to assess pref. shareholders' claim and determines they might be successful and as a result enters into negotiations (para. 15) • Negotiations were successful para. 16: » Amendment to the articles to increase dividend rate (from 8% to 10%) » Right to nominate a director if 3 dividend payments are missed (safety provision) • Brewski agrees to redeem 5% of the shares—to provide addition liquidity to support the market price of the shares • Appellant negotiated protections (i.e., not negligent) para. 17 • Independent directors raised concern about the prudence of the proposed arrangement (para. 19) • De Beers makes the comment about buying back the depressed notes—also veiled threat reminding the Board he is the majority shareholder (para. 20) • Not likely to issue more debt due to lack of capability (para. 21) • De Beers makes the "suds on the face" comment—even though it looks like independent directors expressed having second thoughts (para. 21) • Porter (CEO) announces to noteholder committee • No incidental effects will stop this transaction • Will not be deterred from doing what's in the best interest of the shareholders • No further discussion resulted (para. 23)	as well as he was concerned that this would be viewed as him "hanging on to his playthings" (para. 9) • Based on the professional advice given to them, the Board decided that in order to carry out the spin-off on a tax deferral basis a butterfly transaction is acceptable (para. 10) • P.A. "apparently" was viewed favourably by the market by the 13% increase (para. 11) • Brewski treated the pref. shareholders similarly to the noteholders i.e., they determined their rights were not affected (para. 14) • Arm's length pref. shares objected claiming pref. rights would be affected as it pertains to their rights on liquidation (para. 15) • Negotiations (De Beers was not involved in the negotiations, removed himself from the Board and did not vote in the formal approval) with Brewski and pref. shareholders were successful (paras. 15 and 16) • Brewski gets legal advice to assess pref. shareholders' claim and determine they might be successful and as a result enter into negotiations (para. 15) • Noteholders = sophisticated entity with a floating charge (para. 17) • Proposed arrangement will not breach indenture (para. 17); legal and accounting advice was sought to confirm this (para. 18); it would always pass the solvency test (para.18) • Independent directors raised the concern about the prudence of the proposed arrangement (para. 19) • Board determined on a cost-benefit analysis that the benefit outweighed the downgrade in the rating of the notes (para. 21) • Brewski had no intention to enter the debt market (para. 21)

The Official Rules for the 2009–2010 Harold G. Fox Intellectual Property Moot

PREAMBLE

The Harold G. Fox Moot was founded by Professor Emir A. Crowne-Moham-med and Mohamed Hashim (class of '09), both of the University of Windsor, Faculty of Law, and the partnership of Dimock Stratton LLP. It is named in honour of the late Harold G. Fox, one of Canada's leading intellectual property scholars and advocates.

The Harold G. Fox Moot is sponsored by Dimock Stratton LLP and admin-istered by the IP Moot Committee - a committee of jurists, practitioners, aca-demics and students. The 2009–2010 IP Moot Committee will be co-chaired by Professor Emir A. Crowne-Mohammed and Angela Furlanetto, partner at Dimock Stratton LLP.

The Harold G. Fox Moot is designed to promote the furtherance of educa-tion in the intellectual property field and to provide participants with the oppor-tunity to interact with jurists of the Ontario, Federal and Supreme Courts and with experienced practitioners of intellectual property law.

These rules are designed to provide for fair and proper conduct during the competition. Any questions regarding these rules should be directed to the IP Moot Committee at emir@uwindsor.ca.

DEFINITIONS

As used in the Harold G. Fox Moot, the following terms shall have the corres-ponding meanings:

"Competition" means the Harold G. Fox Intellectual Property Moot Competition; and shall refer to the oral arguments and any/all matters preceding the oral argument (including registration, and factum preparation), as the context dictates.

"IP Moot Committee" means the Intellectual Property Moot Committee described above, or any sub-committee or sub-set thereof.

"Judge" means a person who shall adjudicate the oral advocacy component of the Competition, as further set out in Section 4.

"Law School Contingent" means a team of four (4) students from one Law School - two (2) students paired together as the Appellant Team and two (2) students paired together as the Respondent Team.

"Marker" means a person who shall adjudicate the written advocacy component of the Competition, as further set out in Section 3.

"Participant" means a student registered to compete in the Competition.

"Rules" means the rules, and discretionary guidelines, set out in this document.

"Team" means, subject to Section 2, two (2) students paired together (i.e. either an Appellant Team or a Respondent Team).

1. **Organization of the Competition**

1.1 Administration
   a) The Competition is presented by the IP Moot Committee.
   b) The Preamble shall form part of, and is integral to, a proper interpretation of these Rules.
   c) The Competition shall take place in the English language only.

1.2 Competition Procedures
1.2.1 The Competition shall consist of two (2) general levels: a Preliminary Round or Rounds (which may include, and if so, followed by, a Semi-Final Round), and a Final Round.
   a) The Preliminary Round shall be open to all student teams pursuing an LL.B., J.D., B.C.L, or LL.L. degree in Canada, or elsewhere; and
   b) Advancement through the Competition shall be:
      i. To the Appellant Team and the Respondent Team with the highest Total Team Score(s) in the Preliminary Round, if there is no Semi-Final Round. These two (2) Teams shall advance to the Final Round; or
      ii. Subject to sub-section 8.6, to the two (2) Appellant Teams and the two (2) Respondent Teams with the highest Total Team Score(s) in the Preliminary Round, if there is a Semi-Final Round. These four

(4) Teams will advance to the Semi-Final Round. The Appellant Team and the Respondent Team with the highest Raw Score—Oral in the Semi-Final Round shall then advance to the Final Round; and

b) In the event of a tie pursuant to 1.2.1 (b) ("Tied Teams"), then the Team with the highest Raw Score—Factum (among those Tied Teams) shall advance, and be deemed to have broken said tie.

1.2.2 The Competition shall consist of a written problem in the area of Intellectual Property Law (the "Moot Problem").

1.2.3 Each Team shall draft a written factum (pursuant to section 6).

1.2.4 Each Team shall make one (or a series) of oral arguments during the Competition.

1.2.5 Each Team will act as either the Appellant or the Respondent.

1.3 *Implementation and Interpretation of Rules*

The IP Moot Committee shall serve as the final arbiter for the implementation and interpretation of these Rules.

2.   Participation and Eligibility

2.1 *Team Eligibility*

All students registered in an LL.B., J.D., B.C.L, or LL.L. program in Canada, or elsewhere, are eligible to participate in the Competition (hereinafter, for convenience, the "Law School").

Each Law School participating in the Competition must enter at least one Law School Contingent and may enter up to two (2) Law School Contingents.

Except as provided for in 2.4 *bis*:

a) Each Participant shall either represent the Appellant Team, **or** a Respondent Team; and

b) No Participant shall be allowed to argue, or switch between, Appellant and Respondent Teams; or among Law School Contingents.

2.2 *Team Composition and Selection*

2.2.1 Each Team shall be composed of two (2) Participants. Participants must form their own Teams and be from the same Law School in accordance with 2.1.

2.2.2 At the discretion of the IP Moot Committee, each Team shall be assigned a number (the "Team Number") by the IP Moot Committee. Teams shall use only their Team Numbers for identification purposes during the Competition.

2.2.3 No Team should reveal the actual names of the Participants, or their Law School affiliation, at any time during the Competition. In the interests of fairness to other Teams or Participants, any Team or Participant who violates this rule 2.2.3 may face immediate expulsion from the Competition.

2.3 Outside Assistance to Teams

Subject to 2.4 and 2.5, all research, writing and editing must be the work product of the Team and no one else.

2.4 Assistance from Faculty Members, Coaches and Advisors

Outside assistance rendered to a Team in the preparation of its case by faculty members, sessional lecturers, practitioners, or other members of legal community, shall be limited to a general discussion of the issues, suggestions as to research sources, and consultations regarding oral advocacy technique. Assistance shall be limited to general commentary on argument organization and structure, the flow of arguments, and format.

(2.4 *bis*) Assistance from Other Students

Notwithstanding any of the foregoing, each Law School Contingent may also utilize an additional student Participant (the "Additional Participant") from its Law School. Except for oral arguments on the day(s) of the Competition, the Additional Participant is permitted to perform any of the other activities that other Participants on the Team may be engaged in, including research, peer coaching, and/or factum writing.

The Additional Participant may only engage in oral arguments on the day(s) of the Competition where a Participant on the Law School Contingent, acting in good faith, is unavailable due to some *force majeure*. Upon the occurrence of said *force majeure*, the name of the Additional Participant must be revealed to the IP Moot Committee, in writing, as soon as reasonably possible, having regard to the circumstances. The nature of the *force majeure* must also be documented, if reasonably possible, having regard to the circumstances.

2.5 Assistance from Librarians and Other Research Professionals

Assistance from librarians, computer research advisors, and other legal resource specialists in preparing the Factum, and any other materials, shall be limited to answering specific questions regarding the location of legal sources or general legal research methods.

2.6 Use of Opposing Team's Facta

Subject to 2.6 *bis*, no Team shall be allowed to view or otherwise become privy to any factum other than the respective Appellant and Respondent facta of scheduled opposing Team(s).

(2.6 *bis*) Use of Facta

Each Law School Contingent is permitted to view or otherwise become privy to the factum of that particular Law School Contingent's Appellant and/or Respondent factum in its preparation for the Competition.

Where a Law School is sending two (2) Law School Contingents, then each Law School Contingent from that particular Law School is permitted to view or otherwise become privy to the Appellant and/or Respondent factum of its other Law School Contingent in its preparation for the Competition.

2.7 Withdrawal from the Competition

Given that each Appellant Team in the Competition is reliant upon the production of a factum and presentation of oral arguments by its opposing Respondent Team and *vice-versa*, and but for extenuating circumstances, it is essential that Participants be unable to withdraw from the Competition following the final date of registration.

Any requests for withdrawal from the Competition after the final registration date, shall be subject to the discretion of the IP Moot Committee and may result in an ethical violation.

2.8 Ethical Violations

An ethical violation may result where any Team or Participant acts contrary to the spirit and content of the Rules. Any incidents or allegations of ethical violations shall be referred to the IP Moot Committee. Such violations may result in elimination from the Competition in the current year or in future years, or any other penalty the IP Moot Committee deems appropriate.

3 Factum Markers

3.1 Marker Panels and Selection of Markers

a) Factum Markers shall consist solely of IP Moot Committee members who are not students (the "Marking Panel").

b) Marking Panels may consist of up to five (5) members of the IP Moot Committee, with a view to having at least two (2) members whenever practical.

c) Marking Panels may also be constituted with non-members of the IP Moot Committee at the discretion of the Chair in urgent or unusual circumstances.

d) Marking Panels of one (1) may also be constituted at the discretion of the Chair in urgent or unusual circumstances.

e) All Factum Markers shall act objectively and fairly, and shall maintain the integrity of the Competition at all times.

3.2 Markers Affiliated with Mooters

a) Markers must disqualify themselves from judging a Team:
  (i) if they have a personal or professional relationship with someone affiliated with that Team; **and**

(ii) if that relationship might jeopardize their impartiality, or has a reasonable potential to create bias or impropriety.

b) Markers should not disqualify themselves from judging a round merely because they have an acquaintance with a Team member.

3.3 Commentary by Markers

a) Markers shall not provide any Participant with direct feedback following their moot. Markers shall not reveal to any Participant the results of their individual determinations or the Participant's scoring. All Markers are under a strict obligation of confidence to Participants, and others.

b) All written or oral comments of Markers must be made in good faith, in a professional and constructive manner.

c) Where available, the comments described in 3.3(b) will be released on the conclusion of the Competition or a reasonable time thereafter.

4 Judges

4.1 Judging Panels and Selection of Judges

a) The Judging panels shall consist of a mix of practitioners, IP professionals, professors and judicial judges (altogether, "Judges"). A panel of at least three (3) judges shall be utilized whenever possible for the Preliminary Rounds. Panels of three (3) judges or five (5) judges shall be used to judge the Final Round of the Competition. Deviations from the three (3) judge panel for the Preliminary Rounds shall be approved by the IP Moot Committee, or the Chair in urgent or unusual circumstances.

b) In constituting the Judging panels, priority will be given to judicial judges. As such, some Judging panels may be constituted with more than one judicial judge, even were there are professors or practitioners available.

4.2 Commentary by Judges

Judges in either the Preliminary Round or Final Round of the Competition are encouraged to provide direct feedback (whether written or verbal) to participants regarding their performance at the completion of the Moot or at a time shortly thereafter.

5 The Moot Problem

5.1 Drafting of Moot Problem

The Moot Problem will be drafted by a non-student member of the IP Moot Committee. The IP Moot Committee may invite persons outside of the IP Moot Committee to help draft the Moot Problem, as needed.

5.2 Questions of Clarification

a) Questions of clarification regarding the Moot Problem must be submitted to the IP Moot Committee in writing by November 27th, 2009.

b) Questions cannot relate to the substantive legal issues (or sub-issues), raised by the Moot Problem.

c) In the IP Moot Committee's sole discretion, any question which violates 5.2(b) may not be answered.

6 Facta

6.1 General Requirements and Submission of Facta

a) All facta must conform to the requirements set out in this Section. Teams will be penalized for failure to abide by these requirements.

b) Once submitted to the Competition, facta may not be altered in any way.

c) Once submitted, all rights in and to the facta will become the property of the IP Moot Committee. The IP Moot Committee may seek to have the winning facta published in a legal journal. Subject to any other editorial and publication requirements of the journal in question, authors of the winning facta may be allowed a short period of time to correct mistakes and make revisions prior to any publication.

6.2 Format of Facta

a) Facta must be typed and submitted on white, standard letter size paper (8 ½ by 11 inches).

b) The font and size of the text of all parts of the factum excluding the footnotes, must be the same and must be Times New Roman, 12-point.

c) The font and the size of the text of all parts of the footnote must be Times New Roman, 10-point.

d) The text of all parts of each factum must be double-spaced, except for the text of footnotes and headings which may be single-spaced, but there must be double-spacing between each heading and the body-text of the factum.

e) Quotations to sources of fifty (50) words or more in any part of the factum shall be block quoted (i.e. right and left indented ½ additional inches) and must be single-spaced.

f) Each page of the factum shall have margins of at least one inch, or two point five four (2.54) centimetres, on all sides, excluding page numbers.

6.3 Parts of the Factum

The factum shall consist of the following parts:

- Overview
- Statement of Facts;

- Points in Issue;
- Arguments in Brief;
- Order Requested;
- Table of Authorities; and
- Appendices (if any)

6.4 Citation

Each factum shall adhere to the most current edition of the *Canadian Guide to Uniform Legal Citation.*

6.5 Length

The entire factum (excluding the cover page, table of authorities, and appendices) shall not exceed twenty (20) pages.

6.6 Covers

Each factum should bear on its cover the following, and only the following:

a) the Team number;

b) the name of the court (i.e. the Supreme Moot Court for Intellectual Property Appeals);

c) the appropriate style of cause;

d) the year of the Competition;

e) a one sentence summary of the Moot Problem (e.g. "Appeal concerning enforceability of functional trade-mark rights"); and

f) the title of the document (i.e. "Factum for Respondent" or "Factum for Appellant").

6.7 Number of Facta

a) One (1) electronic copy of each Team's factum must also be submitted to the IP Moot Committee, in a Word or PDF document, at emir@uwindsor.ca; and

b) Within two (2) business days of electronic submission, each Team must submit ten (10) copies of their factum to the IP Moot Committee at the following postal address, during business hours (9 am to 5 pm):

> Angela Furlanetto, Co-Chair of the Harold G. Fox Moot,
> Dimock Stratton LLP,
> 20 Queen Street West, Suite 3202
> Toronto, ON, M5H 3R3

6.8 Submission of Facta

a) In accordance with 2.2.2, Team Numbers shall be assigned by Monday, January 11th, 2010.

b) Pursuant to 6.7, all Appellant facta must be received at that e-mail address by 5:00 pm on Thursday, January 21st, 2010 and at that postal address within two (2) business days of that date. Appellant Teams should request a "delivery receipt" or similar delivery confirmation for their facta—both electronic, and hard-copy—as proof of successful delivery. In the event of a dispute or query, the facta will be deemed "received" upon such proof of successful delivery.

c) The IP Moot Committee will determine Team pairings (i.e. Appellant Team versus Respondent Team) for the initial oral argument(s) during the Preliminary Round, on a random basis, except that the selection process will be conducted with a view to excluding Team pairings from the same Law School Contingent.

d) Following the draw, and as soon as reasonably possible after the Appellant facta are received (but before the Respondent facta is due), the IP Moot Committee will forward the Appellant's factum to that particular Respondent they will be opposing in the initial oral argument(s) during the Preliminary Round.

e) Pursuant to 6.7, the Respondent's facta must be received at that e-mail address by 5:00 pm on Friday, January 29th, 2010 and at that postal address within two (2) business days of that date. Respondent Teams should request a "delivery receipt" or similar delivery confirmation for their facta—both electronic, and hard-copy—as proof of successful delivery. In the event of a dispute or query, the facta will be deemed "received" upon such proof of successful delivery.

7   Oral Argument—Procedures

7.1   General Procedures

a) Each Team's oral argument shall last for thirty (30) minutes.

b) Subject to 7.1(c), each Participant shall be expected to a prepare fifteen (15) minute oral presentation.

c) The Appellant shall be permitted an optional five (5) minute reply submission following the conclusion of the Respondent Team's (i.e. both Participant's) submissions (the "Reply Submission").

7.2   Extension of Time at Judges' Discretion

a) Judges may, at their discretion, extend individual oral argument beyond the fifteen (15) minute allocation, up to an additional five (5) minutes per Participant ("Additional Time").

b) Participants who are permitted this Additional Time are expected to utilize such time to either answer a Judge's question(s) or conclude their submissions.

c) In the spirit of the Competition, and in the interest of allowing each Participant an equal amount of time to present their argument, Judges are strongly admonished to allow each Participant a similar amount of time for oral argument, consistent with these Rules.

d) No Additional Time is permitted for the Reply Submission.

7.3 *Oral Argument*

The order of the oral argument for the Preliminary Round and Final Round of the Competition shall be:

Appellant 1 ▸ Appellant 2 ▸ Respondent 1 ▸ Respondent 2 ▸ Optional Reply Submission from *either* Appellant 1 *or* Appellant 2.

7.4 *Scope of Oral Argument*

A Team's oral argument must be limited to the scope of that Team's factum. A Team may expand upon issues raised in their factum, but the oral arguments must still relate to the written submissions found in the factum.

7.5 Ex Parte *Procedure*

a) In extreme circumstances, such as when a Team fails to appear for a scheduled oral argument, the Marker, after waiting ten (10) minutes, may allow the oral argument to proceed *ex parte*.

b) In an *ex parte* proceeding, the attending Team presents its oral pleading, which is scored by the Marker(s) to the extent possible as if the absent Team had been present and arguing.

c) The Committee may schedule an additional *ex parte* proceeding for the absent Team later in the Competition, if time, administrative concerns, and fairness to other Teams permit, otherwise the absent Team forfeits the Competition.

7.6 *Oral Courtroom Communication and Activity at Counsel Table*

a) Every courtesy shall be given to oralists during oral argument. Subject to 7.7, communication at the counsel table shall be in writing as to prevent disruption, and Teams shall avoid all unnecessary noise, outbursts, or other inappropriate behaviour which distracts from the argument in progress.

b) Any violation of 7.6(a) may be taken into account by the Judges in determining their final score(s).

7.7 *Written Courtroom Communication*

a) Written communication during oral arguments shall be limited to
   1) written communication between a Team's members seated at the counsel table, and
   2) a Team member at counsel table handing an unmarked document to an oralist when that oralist has been questioned about such document during the course of his or her argument.

b) No other written communication may take place among the oralists, Team members seated at counsel table, or spectators.

c) Mobile phone messaging, or the use of portable electronic devices (such as laptops) for the purposes of messaging, shall also be considered forms of "written communication" for the purposes of this section 7.7.

7.8 Spectators
Subject to 7.9, and the availability of space, the Competition is open to the public.

7.9 Scouting
No Participant, except an Additional Participant, may attend any oral argument other than those in which their Team is competing until following completion of the Team's oral argument, or series of oral arguments.

7.10 Audio and Videotaping
The IP Moot Committee reserves all rights to the audio and videotaping, or any other form of aural or visual reproduction, of any oral argument, or part thereof. Pursuant to the registration details of the Competition, all Teams participating have consented to the taping and broadcasting of their oral argument(s).

8.0 Competition Scoring

8.1 Preliminary Round(s)
8.1.1 Subject to 1.2.1(b), scoring shall consist of two parts: (1) the scoring of the written facta, and (2) the scoring of the oral arguments.

8.1.2 All facta shall be reviewed and assigned a score by each Marker on a scale of 5 to 20 points in accordance with the "Marking Guide — Factum" attached as appendix A [here appendix C(i)].

8.1.3. Each Judge shall assign each oralist a score on a scale of 16 to 40 points in accordance with the "Marking Guide — Oral Presentation" attached as appendix B [here appendix C(ii)].

8.2 Raw Scores
Subject to section 9, the calculation of Raw Scores shall be subject to the deduction of Penalty Points.

8.3 Raw Score — Factum
a) The calculation of the "Raw Score — Factum" for each Team shall be determined:
   i) by the Marker's Factum score for that factum, if a single person; or
   ii) by averaging the Markers' Factum scores (if there is more than one Marker, pursuant to section 3) for that factum.

b) The *top factum* will be decided based on the Raw Score—Factum. In the event of a tie, then the Total Score (pursuant to 8.5) shall be used to break that tie.

8.4 *Raw Score—Oral*
a) The calculation of the "Raw Score—Oral" for each Participant shall be determined by averaging the Judges' Oral Presentation scores for that Participant.
b) The *top oralist* will be decided based on the Raw Score—Oral. In the event of a tie, then the Total Score (pursuant to 8.5) shall be used to break that tie.

8.5 *Total Team Score*
The Total Team Score shall be the "Raw Score—Factum" added to the "Raw Score—Oral" for each Participant of the Team, and therefore expressed as a number out of 100.

8.6 *Semi-Final Round*
a) A determination of the Teams that will enter the Semi-Final Round shall be based on a determination of the top two (2) Appellant Teams and top two (2) Respondent Teams as determined by a calculation of the cumulative Total Team Score from the previous preliminary rounds.
b) Where a Law School has two (2) Law School Contingents only a maximum of one (1) Appellant Team and one (1) Respondent Team shall advance to the Semi-Final round—i.e., the Appellant Team with the highest cumulative Total Team Score and the Respondent Team with the highest cumulative Total Team Score.

8.7 *Final Round*
The winning Team for the Competition shall be determined during the Final Round. The winning Team shall be determined solely on the basis of the Raw Score—Oral during the Final Round.

In the event of a tie among the Teams in the Final Round, then the Raw Score—Factum shall be used to break said tie.

9 Penalties

9.1 *General Procedure*
The following is a list of Penalties which may be imposed by the IP Moot Committee upon Participants in the Competition.

9.2 *Application of Penalties*
All Penalties apply against each raw score, e.g. a Penalty of one (1) point shall be applied to the score that *each* Marker or *each* Judge (as applicable) would have given that particular factum or oral pleading.

9.3   *Non-Discretionary Penalties*

a) For the following violations, Penalties may be assessed as a matter of course, without discretion on the part of the Committee, except in rare or extenuating circumstances, or where the application of a non-discretionary penalty would lead to injustice or absurdity, then the Co-Chairs (acting jointly) or the IP Moot Committee may waive or lessen the severity of a penalty.

b) **Non-Discretionary Factum Penalties**—the following Penalties may be imposed only by the IP Moot Committee and may be deducted from each of the individual scores on a Team's factum. The IP Moot Committee shall notify all affected Teams of imposed Penalties prior to the Preliminary Round.

i) **Tardiness in Submitting Facta**—to ensure an equitable distribution of preparation time between Appellants and Respondents, it is essential that all facta be submitted on time. As such, any factum received by IP Moot Committee following the designated submission time shall be subject to a three (3) point penalty per day.

ii) **Other Non-Discretionary Factum Penalties**—penalties shall be assessed for violations of other Rules concerning the facta by reference to the following list:

   I. Violation of sub-section 2.3 (indication of Team identity in factum)—3 points;

   II. Violation of sub-section 6.2 (incorrect formatting of factum (i.e. incorrect font size, or spacing))—1 point per type of violation;

   III. Violation of sub-section 6.5 (excessive length of factum)—2 points per page (or part thereof) over the specified limit;

   IV. Violation of sub-section 6.6 (failure to include necessary information on factum cover (or to utilize incorrect colour of paper per sub-section 6.2))—1 point per type of violation; and

   V. Violation of sub-section 6.7 (failure to submit the required number of facta)—2 points per facta not submitted.

9.4   *Discretionary Penalties*

a) Aside from 9.3, the Committee may assess up to three (3) point Penalties for violations of the following:

i) revisions to the form and substance of the facta, other than as permitted under these Rules; and

ii) inappropriate behaviour of Participants during the Competition.

b) The size of the Penalty shall correspond to the degree of the violation in the judgment of the IP Moot Committee. Discretionary Penalties shall be imposed only by the IP Moot Committee.

c)   Participants may bring potential violations to the attention of the IP Moot Committee, in writing.

9.5   *Notice to Teams*
The IP Moot Committee may notify Teams of the imposition of such Penalties prior to the beginning of the Preliminary Round, if possible; or as soon as practicable if incurred after the beginning of the Preliminary Round or if discovered pursuant to 9.4 (c).

10   Interpretation of Rules

10.1   *General*
Questions concerning the interpretation of these Rules must be submitted to the IP Moot Committee in writing. Clerks and Judges are not authorized to interpret these Rules.

10.2   De Minimis *Rule*
When the impact of an alleged violation of these Rules is so insignificant as to be determined by IP Moot Committee, or the Chair, to be *de minimis*, the IP Moot Committee, or the Chair, may waive the Penalty. Any *de minimis* exception shall be applied evenly to all Teams, to the extent that such an exception reasonably extends to all Teams.

10.3   *Power to Promulgate Additional Measures*
The IP Moot Committee may promulgate such other measures as may be deemed advisable for the orderly conduct, quality, integrity and reputation of the Competition or to correct deficiencies in the Competition. Modifications shall not violate the spirit of these Rules or the best interests of the Competition.

APPENDIX C(i): FACTUM MARKING GUIDE

Team Names: _____

Team #: _____

1. **Stylistic Considerations**
   - Did the factum comply with all formal requirements?
   - Were proper sentence and paragraph structure and sequence used?
   - Did the factum contain grammatical or spelling errors?
   - Was the language clear and comprehensible (effective use of "plain English" principles)?

1   2   3   4

Comments (if Any)

_____

_____

_____

_____

2. **Authorities and Citations**
   - Were sufficient and proper legal citations applied consistently throughout?
   - Did Counsel rely on appropriate and strong authorities?
   - Was a sufficiently broad range of authorities cited?

1   2   3   4

Comments (if Any)

_____

_____

_____

_____

3. **Organization of Issues**
   - Was there a clear and correct statement of the facts and issues?
   - Were the issues organized and did they flow in a logical order?
   - Were the issues discretely divided or were they convoluted?
   - Was there appropriate use of sub-headings, etc.?

1   2   3   4

Comments (if Any)

_____

_____

_____

_____

4. Development of Arguments

- Were the arguments presented in a persuasive and compelling manner?
- Did Counsel apply the correct substantive law in crafting legal arguments?
- Was appropriate weight given to each issue with a focus on Counsel's strongest arguments or were there unnecessary arguments?
- Did Counsel effectively apply the law to the facts?
- Were the arguments creative and/or original or was it merely a restatement of the lower court decisions?

2   4   6   8

Comments (if Any)

_____

_____

_____

_____

TOTAL—FACTUM: _____ /20

APPENDIX C(ii): ORAL PRESENTATION MARKING GUIDE

Presenter: _____

Date/Time/Room: _____

Team #: _____

1. **Speaking Ability and Delivery:**
   - Did Counsel address the bench and opposing Counsel appropriately?
   - Did Counsel interrupt the bench?
   - Did Counsel display appropriate court etiquette in general?
   - Did Counsel make eye contact with the bench?
   - Did Counsel maintain composure under stress?
   - Did Counsel employ appropriate speed and tone in his or her submissions?
   - Was Counsel able to speak from memory or a brief outline or was Counsel reading his or her submissions?

3 4 5 6 7

Comments (if Any)

_____

_____

_____

_____

2. **Organization of Arguments:**
   - Did counsel provide an introduction or "road map"?
   - Were the arguments organized in a logical sequence?
   - Did Counsel sufficiently integrate oral arguments with written arguments?
   - Did Counsel conclude with a concise and effective summary of the arguments?

3 4 5 6 7

Comments (if Any)

_____

_____

_____

_____

3. Questions from the Bench:
- Was Counsel adequately prepared to answer questions from the bench?
- Did Counsel address the issue or were answers evasive?
- Were questions handled properly and did Counsel re-direct the Court's attention back to the issues effectively?
- Did Counsel make concessions where appropriate and in an effective manner?

8   10   12   14   16

Comments (if Any)

_____

_____

_____

_____

4. Preparation & Development of the Arguments:
- Was Counsel sufficiently familiar with the issues?
- Were the arguments developed in a persuasive manner?
- Were concessions made only where necessary and in the proper manner?
- Did Counsel efficiently allocate time among the arguments with a focus on the strongest arguments?
- Did Counsel sufficiently integrate the facts into his or her arguments?
- Did Counsel address and appropriately dispose of opposing Counsel's arguments?

2   4   6   8   10

Comments (if Any)

_____

_____

_____

_____

TOTAL—ORAL PRESENTATION: _____ /40

APPENDIX D

Tips for Drafting a Motion

DRAFTING A MOTION

Introduction

While many first-year moots are conducted as simulated Court of Appeal hearings, some are organized to provide students with the experience of arguing a "motion."

Briefly, a motion involves a request that a decision maker render an order with respect to some aspect of litigation that has been commenced between the parties. The purpose of a motion is quite different from that of an appeal. In the latter case, an entire trial process has generally occurred, and an appeal court is asked to determine whether a sufficiently significant error was made by the trial judge to warrant reversing the judgment or ordering a new trial of the case. A motion, on the other hand, is often undertaken with the purpose of shortening or ending the litigation process.[1] Examples include motions for summary judgment; motions to determine questions of law; motions to compel a person to answer questions during the discovery process; and motions to require parties to produce documents that are relevant to the case. For each, it is important to understand the type of evidence required, and the legal threshold to be met in order to obtain the desired order. Many lawyers in both early and more advanced years of their practice will spend numerous hours in weekly motions court as motions provide a wonderful way to hone written and oral advocacy skills.

---

1   Note, however, that motions can occur after trial. For example, a motion requesting a judge to order a lawyer responsible for some or all of the costs of an action (see, for example, Ontario's *Rules of Civil Procedure*, R.R.O. 1990, Reg. 194, r. 57.07) would occur after trial.

Numerous aspects of mooting a motion replicate those relating to an appeal. Therefore, the "best practices" set out within this book relating to appellate level moots will apply equally to arguing motions. The remainder of this section is therefore devoted to the nature of motions and their general structure.

Procedural Matters

The authority to bring a motion before a (real) court will be found within the procedural rules of the jurisdiction in which one practises. For example, in Ontario, a general outline of motions procedures is provided in rule 37 of the *Rules of Civil Procedure*.[2] Other rules may set out additional requirements for specific types of motions. Likewise, Part 7 of the *Federal Courts Rules*[3] governs the filing of motions before the Federal Court (Canada).

Generally, parties who wish to bring a motion before a court for hearing must make the court aware of this request by way of a written "Notice of Motion." Often, this document will be provided to students to assist them with their preparation for the moot. It is important to pay attention to the Notice of Motion because it outlines the relief being sought by the "Moving Party" and the documentary evidence and authorities to be used on the hearing of the motion. Note that a "Moving Party" can be any party to the overall court action. For example, a Defendant could be the "Moving Party" on a motion to have the Plaintiff's claim dismissed due to the Statement of Claim having been filed after the expiry of the applicable limitation period. The party (or parties) who must respond to the motion is, aptly enough, called the "Responding Party."

The information contained in the Notice of Motion will assist students in drafting a factum in preparation for the argument of the motion, and in organizing that oral argument. A sample Notice of Motion is provided below.

---

2 *Ibid.* For Alberta, see *Alberta Rules of Court*, Alta. Reg. 390/1968, Part 29; for British Columbia, see *Supreme Court Rules*, B.C. Reg. 221/90, r. 44 ("Interlocutory Applications"); for Manitoba, see *Court of Queen's Bench Rules*, Man. Reg. 553/88, rr. 37 and 39; for New Brunswick, see *Rules of Court*, N.B. Reg. 82-73, r. 37; for Nova Scotia, see *Civil Procedure Rules*, r. 22, online: www.courts. ns.ca/rules/toc.htm; for Newfoundland and Labrador, see *Rules of the Supreme Court, 1986*, S.N.L. 1986, c. 42, Sch. D, r. 29 (Applications—Interlocutory Applications); for Northwest Territories and Nunavut, see *Rules of the Supreme Court of the Northwest Territories*, N.W.T. Reg. 010-96, Part 31; for Prince Edward Island, see *Rules of Civil Procedure*, r. 37, online: www.gov. pe.ca/courts/supreme/rules; for Quebec, see *Code of Civil Procedure*, R.S.Q. c. C-25, Part 4; for Saskatchewan, see *Queen's Bench Rules*, Part 38, online: www.qp.gov.sk.ca/documents/English/ Rules/qbrules.pdf; for Yukon, see *Rules of Court*, r. 47 (Applications), online: www.yukoncourts.ca/ courts/supreme/ykrulesforms.html. Note that in some jurisdictions, the term "interlocutory application" is used to refer to the same type of procedure referred to in this chapter as a "motion."

3 S.O.R./98-106.

Court File No. 2008W

OSGOODE
SUPERIOR COURT OF JUSTICE

YANIK BLOOM

Plaintiff

and

JORDY BARK

Defendant

NOTICE OF MOTION

THE Defendant will make a motion to the court as soon as the motion can be heard at Osgoode Hall Law School, 4700 Keele Street, Toronto, Ontario.

PROPOSED METHOD OF HEARING: The motion is to be heard
- ☐ in writing under subrule 37.12(1) because it is on consent, unopposed, or made without notice
- ☐ in writing as an opposed motion under subrule 37.12.1(4);
- ☒ orally.

THE MOTION IS FOR:

1. an order declaring that the Plaintiff commenced this action against the Defendant after the expiry of the two year limitation period prescribed by the *Limitations Act, 2002*, S.O. 2002, c. 24;
2. an order dismissing this action;
3. costs of this motion on a partial indemnity basis; and
4. such other order as this Honourable Court may deem just.

THE GROUNDS FOR THE MOTION ARE:

1. sections 4, 5 and 7 of the *Limitations Act, 2002*, S.O. 2002, c. 24;
2. rules 20 and 21 of the *Rules of Civil Procedure*, R.R.O. 1990, reg. 194; and
3. such further and other grounds as counsel may advise and this Honourable Court may permit.

THE FOLLOWING DOCUMENTARY EVIDENCE WILL BE USED AT THE HEARING OF THE MOTION:

1. Winter 2008 Moot Problem;
2. Waiver from signed by Yanik Bloom dated May 12, 20XX; and
3. such further or other material as counsel may advise and this Honourable Court may permit.

March 20, 2008

Elements of the Motion

Along with the documentary evidence referred to in the Notice of Motion, the mooter will prepare a factum that provides the student with the foundation for your oral argument. Many rules of civil procedure require that a factum be filed as part of the motion; and, even when not required, it is increasingly expected that each party will provide a factum to assist the court in understanding the facts, issues, and law relating to the motion. Do not underestimate the importance of this document. When it is well-crafted and persuasive, a student would have prepared the judges well for oral argument. Providing the bench with a clear understanding of a mooter's position will allow the student to spend less time explaining the basics of her argument, and more time "fleshing" them out and addressing specific aspects of the argument(s) that the judges may seek clarification on. A few reminders about the specific parts of a factum are provided below.

Header

The header is the top section of the first page of the factum, which must include:

1) the court file number, which students should replicate from the court file number found on the Notice of Motion;
2) the name of court in which the motion is being heard;
3) the names and titles of the parties; and
4) the title of the document.

So, following from the Notice of Motion above, the Header for the Moving Party's Factum should be presented as follows:

Court File No. 2008W

OSGOODE
SUPERIOR COURT OF JUSTICE

YANIK BLOOM

Plaintiff

and

JORDY BARK

Defendant

Factum of the (Defendant) Moving Party, Jordy Bark

The header for the Responding Party will be almost identical, the only difference being the title of the document.

OSGOODE
SUPERIOR COURT OF JUSTICE

YANIK BLOOM

Plaintiff

and

JORDY BARK

Defendant

Factum of the (Plaintiff) Responding Party, Yanik Bloom

PART I: OVERVIEW

While overview paragraphs are not generally required, they are becoming increasingly common. The purpose of an overview section is to contextualize (and humanize) for the reader the facts and law sections that follow. One Court of Appeal judge has written, "I did not write an overview paragraph when I prepared my own factums. Now I think it is an essential element of a good factum."[4]

Students should ensure that it is acceptable to include an overview in the moot competition's rules. If it is, students should briefly provide the following: (1) the nature of the motion (what the court hearing the motion is being asked to do); (2) a brief indication of how the motion relates to the overall proceedings (remember that a motion is not a "stand alone" proceeding—it is linked to an existing court action); (3) a summary of the mooter's position (and their notional "client") with respect to the motion; and (4) a brief "motivating statement" about what is at stake in these proceedings—what it is that should make a court want to rule in the mooter's favour. It is a judge's primary role to promote justice between the parties and, in a broader sense, for society. The most persuasive emphasis for any given motion will, of course, depend on the circumstances of the party a mooter represents.

In the *Bloom v. Bark* example above, the Moving Party, who is the defendant in a negligence claim, will want to argue that it is unfair for the Moving Party to be subject to a court action after the statutorily-enacted time limit for commencing a legal action has expired. His overview paragraph might read as follows:

> [#]   The Moving Party, Jordy Bark ["Mr. Bark"] seeks to have the action of the
> Plaintiff, Yanik Bloom ["Ms. Bloom"], dismissed. The claim that Mr. Bark's acts
> or omissions led to the Plaintiff sustaining injuries during a horseback riding les-

---

4   The Honourable Justice John I Laskin, "The View from the Other Side: What I Would Have Done Differently if I Knew Then What I Know Now" (Spring 1998) 17:2 Advocates' Soc. J. at 17.

son should be dismissed because the two-year limitation period applicable to tort actions in Ontario has expired. The Plaintiff knew or reasonably ought to have known that she had a claim against him on the date of the accident in question, and by not pursuing the claim within two years after that date, the law has proscribed her action and it is now statute-barred. Defendants should not be subject to indeterminate periods of potential liability.

The Responding Party's overview would be similar to the Moving Party's overview in the way that it describes the motion and the overall action. The key differences, of course, relate to the Responding Party's position with respect to the motion, and the motivating statement in support of that position.

[#] This is a motion by the Defendant, Jordy Bark ["Mr. Bark"], for the dismissal of the negligence action brought by the Plaintiff, Yanik Bloom ["Ms. Bloom"], in relation to injuries she sustained during a horseback riding lesson that Mr. Bark was supervising. The Plaintiff opposes the motion. The two-year limitation period relied on by the Defendant in support of the motion has not expired. In light of the nature of the injuries sustained, Ms. Bloom did not know, and could not have reasonably known, that she had a claim against the Defendant on the date of the accident in question. The action was commenced within two years of the date that Ms. Bloom could reasonably have known of such a claim.

The Defendant here is emphasizing the underlying policy of statutory limitation periods (namely, the endless threat of litigation in perpetuity). The Plaintiff, on the other hand, is emphasizing the need for the limitation period (or limitation clock) to start running from the time she discovered the injury, and not the date the injury itself occurred. Indeed, each overview statement sets the stage for the remainder of that party's factum.

PART II: FACTS

With numbered paragraphs that follow the overview paragraph(s), set out the facts that relate to the determination of the legal issues, or the facts that are necessary to help the client's problem make sense to the reader. Each key fact should be contained in a separate paragraph, with the original source of this fact found listed below it. This is the mooter's opportunity to frame her story in a manner that assists the judge to understand the persuasive value of her position. The writer should think carefully about the way that the facts are presented, keeping in mind that it is essential to be accurate in the representation of the facts. Consider the same basic fact as framed by each party below. The Moving Party wishes to highlight the Plaintiff's own role in the accident's occurrence while emphasizing his positive acts, while the Responding Party wishes to highlight the Defendant's alleged improper supervision and the fall itself.

[Moving Party]

[#]   Due to a lack of proper equipment, and before Mr. Bark could remedy the situation, the horse Ms. Bloom was riding became out of control.

Winter 2008 Moot Problem **at para. 2.**

[#]   Mr. Bark instructed Ms. Bloom to perform an emergency dismount. In performing the dismount, Ms. Bloom struck her head on the ground.

[Responding Party]

[#]   Ms. Bloom, having mounted her horse bareback, was not immediately instructed by Mr. Bark that she must cease riding until he was satisfied that she had saddled the horse properly and attached its bridle.

Winter 2008 Moot Problem **at paras. 1–2.**

[#]   The horse escaped Ms. Bloom's control and she was forced to perform an emergency dismount. During the dismount, she struck her head on the ground.

Winter 2008 Moot Problem **at para. 3.**

In both cases, the facts describe roughly the same circumstances, but each provides a slightly different context for the reader to consider as they move to the next section of the factum. Consider how different word choices might have changed the level of persuasiveness of each sentence. When crafting a factum, both the facts section and the other parts of the document will need to be revised several times to ensure that optimal persuasiveness is achieved.

PART III: LAW AND ARGUMENT

The law and argument section of a factum highlights the blending of facts and law that underpins the mooter's—and their client's—position. Some procedural rules provide that the factum should set out only the law that is relevant to the relief requested. Others provide that a statement of both the law and the related argument should be presented. Even in the former case, however, one will often see the statement of law framed in a manner that suggests the underlying argument in the case.

Again, consecutive paragraph numbers are used in this section, following from the numbering within the facts section. Essentially, the law and argument part of the factum allows the writer to continue to develop the "theory of the motion" being presented on behalf of the client. A persuasive theory is an analysis of the facts and law—intertwined together—that justifies a decision in the client's favour and motivates a court to make that decision.

As mooters build the law and argument section, ensure that each separate point includes a concise statement of the legal principle relied on, an indication of the related facts, and your position about how the law and facts interact. In some cases, students may be able to combine each of these elements into one paragraph. More often, a few paragraphs will be required to develop each point. Below each paragraph, students must provide proper citations for the authorities and facts referred to in that paragraph.

The paragraphs below illustrate the way the Responding Party builds the point that there is ambiguity with respect to when Ms. Bloom ought to have become aware of the link between the riding accident in question and the headaches she was suffering, and that legal authority supports the position that where such ambiguity exists, a case should not be dismissed on the basis of an alleged limitation period expiry.

[#]   As a university student, Ms. Bloom was subject to stress, which can cause headaches on its own. Moreover, physical evidence of her injury was only found when she was examined by a specialist. The specialist also suggested that her symptoms were aggravated by stress. These circumstances made precise discoverability difficult.

Winter 2008 Moot Problem at para. 6.

[#]   The combination of causes (stress and injury) that contributed to Ms. Bloom's headaches introduces significant ambiguity into whether and when Ms. Bloom knew of an actionable claim. Such ambiguity should not be dealt with by a motion to dismiss the action.

Munshaw v. Economical Mutual Insurance Co. (2007), 45 M.V.R. (5th) 111, 48 C.C. L.I. (4th) 43 at paras. 13–16 (Sup. Ct. J.) (WLeC).

Within the factum, it may be tempting to include every possible argument that can be conjured up. Students must resist this temptation, and include only points with a reasonable possibility of persuading the court. Present one's best points, while addressing the issues.

PART IV: RELIEF REQUESTED

When a student has developed all of the viable arguments on behalf of the party she is representing, the factum should conclude with a section setting out a succinct reiteration of how the mooter wishes the court to rule on the motion. Students should also, in most cases, present their client's position regarding the costs of the motion. Finally, in most jurisdictions, students should finish with the line "ALL OF WHICH IS RESPECTFULLY SUBMITTED," followed by their signature and an indication of the party they represent.

Note the differences in Moving Party and Responding Party "Relief Requested" sections below.

[Moving Party]

[#]   The Defendant, Jordy Bark, respectfully requests:

(1) an Order declaring that this proceeding was commenced after the expiry of the applicable two year limitation period;

(2) an Order dismissing this action; and

(3) an Order granting the Defendant costs on a partial indemnity basis.

ALL OF WHICH IS RESPECTFULLY SUBMITTED this 20th day of March, 20XX.

—————————————————

XY

Counsel for the Defendant (Moving Party)

[Responding Party]

[#]   The Plaintiff, Yanik Bloom, respectfully requests:

(1) an Order dismissing the motion; and

(2) an Order granting the Plaintiff costs on a partial indemnity basis.

ALL OF WHICH IS RESPECTFULLY SUBMITTED this 25th day of March, 20XX.

—————————————————

YZ

Counsel for the Plaintiff (Responding Party)

Note that the Moving Party has reiterated the relief requested initially in the Notice of Motion. The Responding Party simply asks that the motion be dismissed. It is not appropriate for the Responding Party to seek any additional relief (other than the costs associated with the Moving Party's motion).

A list of authorities cited in accordance with a prescribed guide to legal citation is included at the end of the factum. If students have been asked to provide a back page in accordance with the applicable rules of procedure, ensure that the required format is followed.

Additional Readings

Ian Binnie, "In Praise of Oral Advocacy" (March 2003) 21:4 Advocates' Soc. J. 3.

Norman Birkett, "The Art of Advocacy" (1947) 25 Can. Bar Rev. 1043.

Marvin Catzman, "The Wrong Stuff: How to Lose Appeals in the Court of Appeal" (August 2000) 19:1 Advocates' Soc. J. 1.

*Maureen Fitzgerald, *Legal Problem Solving: Reasoning, Research and Writing,* 4th ed. (Toronto: Butterworths, 2007).

Bryan Garner & Antonin Scalia, *Making Your Case* (St. Paul, MN: Thomson West, 2008).

*Suzanne Gordon & Sherifa Elkhadem, *The Law Workbook: Developing Skills for Legal Research and Writing* (Toronto: Emond Montgomery, 2001).

Edward L. Greenspan, Sir Sydney Kentridge, & Justice W. Ian Binnie, *The Dubin Lectures on Advocacy* (Aurora: Canada Law Book, 2004).

Christopher Kee, *The Art of Argument* (New York: Cambridge University Press, 2006).

*Margaret E. McCallum, Deborah A. Schmedermann, & Christina L. Kunz, *Synthesis: Legal Reading, Reasoning and Writing in Canada* (Toronto: CCH Canadian, 2003).

*Richard K. Neumann, Jr., *Legal Reasoning and Legal Writing: Structure, Strategy and Style,* 4th ed. (New York: Aspen, 2001).

David Stockwood & David Spiro, eds., *Ethos, Pathos, and Logos: The Best of The Advocates' Society Journal 1982–2004* (Toronto: Irwin Law, 2005).

*Ted Tjaden, *Legal Research and Writing*, 2d ed. (Toronto: Irwin Law, 2004).

*John Yogis *et al.*, *Legal Writing and Research Manual*, 5th ed. (Toronto: Butterworths, 1994).

* These are just some of the many excellent works on factum preparation (and legal writing in general) already aimed at law students.

Glossary

60/40 Rule
A general rule concerning the allotment of time for a mooter's submissions (the "sixty" represents the percentage of time allocated for submissions, whereas the "forty" represents the time allocated for questions from the bench).

Appellant
The party in a moot problem that launches the appeal resulting in the "moot."

Bench brief
A memorandum prepared by the organizers of a moot that distils the moot problem to its bare essentials; it often contains relevant case law, potential arguments and sample questions for panellists to ask.

Cold Bench
A panel of judges that will rarely ask a student questions during oral submissions.

Hard Panel
An intentionally difficult practice panel.

Hot Bench
A panel of judges that continuously asks questions during oral submissions.

Inflection
The tonal increase (or decrease) in a mooter's voice.

Leader
A student from within a moot team that inevitably emerges to guide the moot team's priorities, deadlines, and standards (generally a senior student with extensive moot experience).

Moot coaches

Professors or practitioners who assist in the selection and training of moot teams.

Moot problem

A fictitious scenario, or an appeal of an already decided case, that serves as the basis for the moot competition.

Moot team

One or more students representing a (fictional) Appellant, and one or more students representing a (fictional) Respondent.

Mooting

An academic exercise where students assume the role of legal counsel in a mock trial, appeal, motion, or other hearing.

My friend(s)

A term used by a mooter to refer to the opposing moot team.

Off-book

Presenting submissions without a scripted or verbatim recitation of printed materials.

Order sought

The crux of the mooter's submissions, specifically, the broad threshold remedy or "justice" being sought.

Peer coaching

The use of members of the moot team or other students to preside over practice moots.

Respondent

The party in a moot problem that is most recently successful and receives the appeal from the Appellant.

Right of reply

An optional allotment of time given to the appellant after the Respondent has presented its submissions (sometimes known as a rebuttal).

Road map

An itemization of the mooter's submissions.

Rule of Three

A rule that mooters should present no more than three main points of argumentation during submissions.

Submissions

The oral argument(s) raised by mooters.

Tunnel vision

Fixating on a single panel member during a moot (usually the chief justice).

Waldo

The core theme or narrative a student must develop when presenting his or her submissions, and/or the overall message that distils a party's main argument to a phrase or ideal.